A MARC CORPORATION BOOK

This series in Urban and Ethnic Affairs is sponsored by the Metropolitan Applied Research Center, Inc., Kenneth B. Clark, President.

OTHER MARC CORPORATION BOOKS

A Relevant War Against Poverty, Kenneth B. Clark and Jeannette Hopkins

W. E. B. Du Bois: A Reader, edited and with an introduction by Meyer Weinberg

Racism and American Education, Harold Howe, Kenneth B. Clark, James E. Allen *et al.*

White Terror: The Ku Klux Klan Conspiracy and Southern Reconstruction, Allen W. Trelease

The Black Image in the White Mind: The Debate on Afro-American Character and Destiny 1817–1914, George M. Fredrickson

Aztlan: An Anthology of Mexican American Literature, edited by Luis Valdez and Stan Steiner. New York: Alfred A. Knopf, Inc., 1972

THE WAY

▲▲▲▲▲▲▲▲▲▲▲▲▲▲▲▲▲▲▲▲▲▲▲▲

THE WAY

▼▼▼▼▼▼▼▼▼▼▼▼▼▼▼▼▼▼▼▼▼▼▼▼

An Anthology
of American Indian
Literature

EDITED BY
SHIRLEY HILL WITT AND
STAN STEINER

Alfred A. Knopf   New York   1972

THIS IS A BORZOI BOOK
PUBLISHED BY ALFRED A. KNOPF, INC.

Library of Congress Cataloging in Publication Data

Witt, Shirley Hill, comp.
  The way; an anthology of American Indian literature.

  1. Indian literature—Translations into English.
I. Steiner, Stanley, joint comp.   II. Title.
PM197.E1W5 1972b   897   73–171156
ISBN 0–394–47370–1

Manufactured in the United States of America

FIRST EDITION

CONTENTS

II. SONGS OF THE PEOPLE

IV. "MY TEACHER IS A LIZARD": EDUCATION AND CULTURE

V. THE LAWS OF LIFE: TRIBAL AND LEGAL

VI. THE RITUAL OF DEATH: WAR AND PEACE

VIII. PROPHECIES OF THE FUTURE

High on a hill, overlooking the famed Plymouth Rock, stands the statue of our good sachem, Massasoit. Massasoit has stood there many years in silence. We, the descendants of this great sachem, have been a silent people. The necessity of making a living in this materialistic society of the white man has caused us to be silent. Today, I and many of my people are choosing to face the truth. We are Indians.

Speech by Frank James, of the Wampanoag tribe, Thanksgiving Day, 1970, at Plymouth Rock, Massachusetts, invited, then banned, by officials of the State of Massachusetts.

LISTEN TO HIS MANY VOICES:
AN INTRODUCTION TO THE LITERATURE
OF THE AMERICAN INDIAN

by Shirley Hill Witt

On a ship's prow; at the tobacconist's; in the Smithsonian; on an advertisement for a cigarette, a whiskey for executives—there he stands: the wooden Indian, solemn and humorless, his mouth clamped shut. The mute Indian—as familiar an image as Aunt Jemima, Charlie Chan, and the Frito Bandito.

Yet, he is different from them. For one thing, he has no name. Is he Injun Joe, or Lonesome Polecat? Who is he? He doesn't say: he's mute.

The nameless, mute wooden Indian comes down to us through the years, an old acquaintance. Only Tonto rivals him as the ethnic stereotype, now that Indianhead nickels are so rare. Poor Tonto, whose name means "silly" or "foolish"—his cartoonist was no artist. No face comes to mind, only a brown suit with fringes.

Why a nameless mute image as a legacy for a hundred-thousand year investment in this hemisphere?

Let us see what produced our wooden Indian.

The carvers of this genre of statuary must have shared some prevalent conviction with the public—that there was something mute and wooden about live Indians, those Indians still left when the art form flourished in the late nineteenth century. Have you ever seen a wooden Indian smiling? No.

The artisan and the customer partook of a community of ideas which said that, to be acceptable, the finished product—the statue—must have wild-bird feathers on its head, tomahawk at the ready, enlarged sclera, animal-skin clothes, and mouth clamped shut—no smile. An eagle nose and a vast expanse of upperlip stamped it "Indian."

Were the Indians, in fact, or, at least, impressionistically, silent? Or, were the Indians seen as stupid? East of the Mississippi at the time of the carvings, the miserable remnants of tribes must have been a sorry lot. What is left over after genocide?

Perhaps we could call him "Lo," i.e., Lo, the poor Indian. After all, the Indians had to be stupid since they had lost a whole continent. They had folded up before a superior force of numbers and weaponry. And, then, if non-Indians were superior, Indians were inferior, and they would be stupid, mute. Like our friend, the wooden Indian.

But the whites of his eyes glitter yet. Might this betoken something else, something more than unmitigated stupidity?

Euramericans in the late 1700's and early 1800's were notably ambivalent about their usurpation of a continent and the death of its original inhabitants. On the one hand, the Indian was considered a benighted half-human impeding the God-ordained progress of civilization. On the other hand, he was viewed as the Noble Savage, the epitome of simplicity of man in nature. Montaigne characterized the Indians as bearers of savage goodness, a nation which: "hath no kind of traffic, no knowledge of letters, no intelligence of numbers, no name of magistrate, nor of politics, nor of service, of riches or of poverty; no contracts, no successions, no partitions, no occupation but idle; no apparel but natural, no manuring of lands, no use of wine. . . . The very words that import a lie, a falsehood, treason, covetousness, envy, detraction were never heard among them. . . . Furthermore, they lived in a country of so exceedingly pleasant and temperate situation, that as my testimonies have told me, it is very rare to see a sick body amongst them. . . . They spend the whole day in dancing. The young men go ahunting after wild beasts with bows and arrows. Their women busy themselves therewhilst. . . . We may then well call them barbarous, in regard of reason's rules, but not in respect of us that exceed them in all kinds of barbarism."

Erasmus developed the concept further. In his essay, *In Praise of Folly*, he described Indians as: ". . . the simple people of the golden age . . . furnished with no school knowledge. Nature alone sufficed to guide them; instinct to prompt them how to live. . . . What would have been the advantage of jurisprudence to men among whom bad morals—the sole apology for good laws—had no existence? It is clear to you, I presume, now that those who make wisdom their study, by doing so, make themselves the most miserable of mankind. . . . By the immortal gods, then, I solemnly swear to you that no class of men is happier than that of those whom the world calls simpletons, fools, and blockheads."

Rousseau, Goldsmith, Wordsworth, Coleridge, Dryden, Southey, and Shelley; all these standardized and glorified the Noble Savage, the serenely ignorant creature left over from a golden age.

Now the Noble Savage is the paladin of the tobacco store, placidly offering a handful of cigars while children wheel about him like crows about a scarecrow. He has been tamed and put to use. No longer a child of nature, a superior way has prevailed over him and a superior people make use of him for their own purpose. He submits to the work ethic, to him the self-devouring Manifest Destiny of Western civilization.

Intertwined with the concept of the Noble Savage—inexplicably—is the character trait of stoicism. In the face of all adversity, through all manner of misfortune, the man of nature endures without complaint. Strong. Silent. Wooden.

Could it possibly be that stoicism—not stupidity—had muted the Indian? What was it like to be raped by civilization?

Colonel Richard Irving Dodge wrote a delightful essay on the matter of Indian stoicism in his *The Plains of the Great West*, printed first in 1876. Colonel Dodge was a professional Indian-killer for the U.S. Army, but in that incomprehensible compartmentalization of which Euramerican minds are capable, he was not an Indian-hater. He observed that one shows surprise at something out of the ordinary line of one's experience, whether one is white, Indian, or whatever. "An act of comparison," he called it. Considering the vast number and variety of alien things he was being exposed to during the white invasion, the Indian would be a simple exclamation point if he showed surprise at everything new to him, or everything which he did not understand. Rather, he went to the other extreme, and would rarely show or feel surprise at anything, he said.

Colonel Dodge tells an anecdote:

Twenty years ago, when Indians knew comparatively little of the wonders of civilization, Lieutenant (now General) P_____ was sent with a small force to treat with a band disposed to be troublesome. He took with him as guide and interpreter a Delaware chief, Black Beaver, a warrior celebrated throughout the length and breadth of the plains. Beaver was semi-civilized, had been to Washington, owned a farm, and was a person of social consequence in his country. The refractory Indians were assembled in council, and the difficulties adjusted. Lieut. P_____ then proceeded to descant upon the numbers and power of the whites and the folly of the Indians making war upon them. As a peroration, he directed Beaver to tell the Indians about steamboats. Beaver had seen steamboats, and gave a glowing description. At its conclusion a murmur ran through the council. "What do they say, Beaver?" asked P_____. "He say he don't b'lieve that d_____d lie," said Beaver. "Tell them about railroads, then." Beaver had travelled on railroads, so he proceeded to give his ideas and experiences on that subject. Again a murmur passed through the assembly. "What do they say now, Beaver?" asked P_____. "He say he don't b'lieve that d_____d lie either." Somewhat nonplussed for a wonderful thing which they *might* believe, P_____ at last said, "Tell them about the telegraph." "I don't know what that is," answered Beaver. P_____ explained that by the aid of a little wire he could stand where he was and talk to the Great Father at Washington, and etc., etc. Beaver listened attentively, but with a grave face, and made no attempt to translate. "Why don't you tell them?" said P_____, impatiently. " 'Cause," said Beaver, nodding his head slowly and emphatically, " 'cause I don't b'lieve that d_____d lie myself."

One might wonder what these people had left of their faith in themselves, when all they had accomplished and all that they knew came to nothing before superior numbers and weaponry. What other posture, what other stance was left to them other than the wooden face of a will to survive? If all that makes a man a man to his people lies crushed and bloody before him, what other choice remains but to stand mute and enduring?

Sometimes this stoicism is equated with pride and sometimes pride is called stoicism. The "proud Indian" is heard often enough. Indians speak of it themselves as frequently as anyone else, probably. As did the slack-jawed gasp of amazement give way to clamped-mouthed stoicism, somehow stoicism—sheer survival—became equated with pride. And, all along, stupefaction, stoicism, and pride led to only one thing: the mute wooden Indian image.

No writing systems comparable with Old World systems had been developed in the New World. No evidence of formal traditional literature met the eye of the invader—no books, no libraries. The Euramericans found no books to admire nor books to burn. Surely these were a mute people!

But, the typification of the Indian as wooden and mute is, from the native viewpoint, an absurdity. Even Colonel Dodge had time enough between punitive expeditions to learn that, "In their everyday life Indians are vivacious, chatty, fond of telling and hearing stories, indulge in broad wit, and are specially fond of practical jokes."

The fact is, Indians are downright garrulous in comfortable situations, in the proper places. Anyone who has ever attended an Indian conference already knows the truth of this statement.

And there is more to this than sheer talkativeness as opposed to muteness. Simply saying that Indians at home have always been, and still are, loquacious does not lead us any closer to what this book is about. We need to know the traditions which even now dictate the quality and quantity of Indian speech. We need to know something of the antecedents leading to the words this book contains.

Without an effective writing system, man seems yet to feel a need for some kind of perfected communication mode or technique. Man must educate his children with the knowledge of their forebears; he needs to elevate ordinary communication to levels of importance whenever necessary; he needs recreation through verbal communication. These in literate societies can take special and different forms beyond the ordinary.

Depending upon oral transmission for all things, high value is placed on exact repetition of traditional lore, stories, ceremonial narrative, and various parts of governmental business. Among Indians, this is carried further into the realm of everyday life in songs and the repeating of conversations, incidents, anecdotes, jokes, and the like. The tradition of exact repetition persists to the present day in such a way that, for instance, a joke told in New Mexico may be heard again in Nebraska and Indiana and then in Washington, D.C., told by four different Indians, months apart, and yet the joke will be recited exactly, word for word. This contrasts with people who place value on individual improvisation. Appalachian hill people, for instance, try to put a personal stamp on each telling or singing so that the song "Barbara Allen," as an example, has a nearly infinite number of versions. The tradition of exact repetition is not a function of an unimaginative people: It is a tradition born out of necessity for a better recording system.

The tradition has other ramifications which contrast with literate societies. For one, Indian people have a vast respect for the worth of the spoken or written word. The spoken word contains a life all its own, an endless life. The spoken word does not fall to the ground, shatter, and turn to dust, in Indian comprehension. The spoken word is born, takes flight, and lives forever—always ready to be recalled if need be. And, when words have the value of immortality, one is careful not to use them haphazardly or falsely. In contrast, Indian people often harbor an abiding wonder at the blatant lies voiced by advertising, newspapers, politicians, and BIA employees. All words being immortal, are these liars not haunted?

If words possess sanctity and imperishability, they must

be fittingly couched and exhibited. For speech to have full meaning, it must also have silence. Silence is half of speech: speech is half of silence. It is not pause. Neither is it an interlude of anxiety glowing red and viscous. It is not a time of frantic groping for thoughts and words to express thoughts. Least of all is silence the brackets surrounding communication. Silence is the continuity which integrates ideas and words. And it is more. Silence is a thing of power. Beyond any utterance, the power of silence stands vast and awesome.

The power of silence heightened the speech of the ancients even as it does today among the living generations. Such a bountiful style is slow to be abandoned. Thus, it is understood that one must not flood the air with words, hoping that from sheer volume the pristine thoughts will voluntarily float free and full-blown. Only verbal pollution results from this. If we recognize the value of words, then silence is not threatening; it is not laden with tension. Silence instead is potent and honorable.

In the great reluctance of Indian people to interrupt when another person is speaking one sees this respect for words. Only rarely, perhaps in emergencies, does one speak over the voices of others. Part of the reason must simply be what constitutes good manners. But, beyond this, the worth of the word is extended to encompass the right of the individual to speak his own words without interference.

The mark of a traditionalist in speaking is his extreme care in the choice of words he uses, whether it be English or his own language. Linked to the immortality of words is the need to use the precise word needed to express the idea. Often, then, when using English, the listener should conjure up the dictionary definitions of the words he hears rather than apply the looser usages he accepts from other English-speakers. Also this implies, frequently enough, a great economy of a sort in the use of words. A proper speaker will use as few words as possible to convey a specific thought. This does not mean that Indian speeches are short. On the contrary, they seem all too often interminable for non-Indian members of an audience. But each thought is described with a minimum of verbiage. This leads to almost habitual use among traditionalists, who seek to preserve the old ways, of the figure of speech called by the Greeks *synecdoche*. The speaker can hereby designate a part for the whole of a thing (my *wool* for my *sheep herd*), the whole for a part (the *tribe* for the *tribal chairman*), the species for the genus (my *case worker* for the *Bureau of Indian Affairs*), the genus for the species (*Washington* for the *Bureau of Indian Affairs local agency*), the name of the material for the thing made (the *electric* for any *electrical appliance*), and the like. It can become exceedingly complex.

Further, it can often enough provoke massive frustration in those who do not share a body of experiences and certain presumptions with the speaker. In a poem by Simon Ortiz, we are told about the poet's giving a ride to a Navajo woman hitching home. She says she has been to Phoenix to visit her daughter and that "I got a headache." The poem continues right on without pause, because that was the way it was. But the "headache" should convey essays to us, essays about cities and heat and smog and too many people and walk/don't walk signs and mechanical noises and, and, and. This example seems simple enough when it is thought about. But in continuing speech or conversation, the "dichotomy of simple words and cosmic meanings," as Stan Steiner puts it, coming frequently, can sorely press a newcomer.

The most important function of the oral tradition is seen in its official executors—the tribal teachers, the priests, the orators. Not much need be said about these Indian teachers and priests here beyond the fact that their "library" is what they have committed to memory. The orator, on the other hand, combines memorization with the creative talent to articulate well the thoughts and opinions of the people, whether speaking to them or to outsiders. In large part because of this creativity, the orator is a highly respected member of Indian societies. Orating long ago became an art form for these people. The names of many of these orators —often called prophets—come down to us through history. Some whose words we will read here are: Red Jacket, Tecumtha, Black Hawk, Sitting Bull, Seathe, Geronimo. . . .

Thomas Jefferson, in his *Notes On Virginia*, commented on the eloquence of one such orator—Logan, the Mingo chief: "I may challenge the whole orations of Demosthenes and Cicero, or any more eminent orator . . . to produce a single passage superior to the speech of Logan."

In their own turn, the great speeches became part of the oral tradition. The art lives on. The talent and brilliance of a good orator still evokes respect. But, there is a difference between speechmaker and orator. The number of speeches made by Indian speechmakers per year is enormous—and uncountable. Perhaps no other group in North America comes anywhere near the ratios of speeches per capita and speakers per capita as are produced from the ranks of the Indian people. But an orator is something apart: a resource, an asset, a credit to his people.

Five generations of orators are living today and, even if they do not view themselves as traditional orators, others consider them so. Heading the list as perhaps the eldest is Clinton Rickard (Tuscarora). We will name a few others: Vine Deloria, Sr. (Sioux), Paul Bernal (Taos), Wendell Chino (Apache), Robert Lewis (Zuñi), Edward LaPlante (Chippewa), Clifton Hill (Creek), Eugene Crawford (Sioux), Herbert Blatchford (Navajo), Simon Ortiz (Acoma), William

Personeau (Ponca). Of all, Clyde Warrior (Ponca) would have led this list as the best of the young traditionalists. But we have lost him.

Most of those named speak articulately in two languages: English and their own. Many more unknown to outsiders are orators solely in their own languages.

To fault or credit the Iroquois, it was they who caused the English forces to prevail over the French and thus secure the English language for North America. Until this definitive event, two Babels were confronting each other along the flood tide of the frontier.

The Americans embraced a bewildering array of widely diverse languages. Adjacent tribes very often used tongues unintelligible to their neighbors. Bilingualism and multilingualism was well-nigh essential for trade and other intertribal business among Indians for centuries. Several sign languages were developed to overcome linguistic barriers.

And then came Old World peoples with their myriad tongues. Even though English may have been the official language after the French and Indian War, it was not the national language—immigrants spoke whatever language they brought with them, although it may well have been incomprehensible to both their European and Indian neighbors.

No wonder most communication between Indians and Euramericans was relegated to weapon-point! No wonder the Indian seemed mute, wooden. Perhaps he was.

So we have come the circle, from the mute nameless wooden Indian to the tradition of oral literature and its ramifications. And we come now to this anthology.

Two kinds of writing are presented here. First, there are ancient speeches of honored leaders and orators. These must be read for the thoughts they contain rather than for the way in which they are written. Many are second or even third translations. They come to us in flowery old English: "O, Great White Father, we your children. . . ." We do not know whether this formal style was a European or an Indian invention. However, we suspect that, because of its pervasiveness, it might have been the interpreters' idea of a fitting style. Nothing apparent in contemporary Indian speeches and demeanor toward governmental figures suggests this odd style of delivery.

"It is evident that the best translations of Indian oratory must fail to express the beauty and simplicity of the originals," wrote a Mr. Ogden of the Ogden Land Company, after he had been bested in debate by the Seneca orator Sagoyewatha (Red Jacket). "I can give no adequate idea of the strong impression it [Sagoyewatha's oratory] made on my mind, though conveyed through the medium of an illiterate interpreter. Even in this mangled form, it was a splendid oration."

All the U.S. Bureau of American Ethnology native texts should be retranslated, without a doubt.

The second kind of writing found in this anthology is contemporary. It includes both speeches and written articles. Looking through these selections, it should be apparent that two separate forms, spoken and written, are not used by Indians. All is "spoken." Here is a clear survival of an oral tradition: Anything written "reads" well aloud. In fact, the words are mentally "said," then written down. Here, we think, is a distinct contrast with most other English writing. "Hearers," not "readers," are the audience. This is very old. It is also very new.

Taken as a whole, then, what is this volume about?

You are soon to meet Indian thoughts as they were meant to be understood and have not been. You are to experience Indian logic as it naturally flows. You will witness the coalescence of America's ancient, original tradition with present-day language and problems. Indian people will speak to you directly: Their ideas will no longer be veiled by outside interpretation. You may not like the thoughts you perceive, but these are only the first robins of an Indian literary spring, at long last released from a winter of silence. The summer promises to be hot. The mute wooden Indian is vanished. At last, the thoughts and words of the American Indian may be heard throughout his own land. Will you listen to his many voices?

▲▲▲▲▲▲▲▲▲▲▲▲▲▲▲▲▲▲▲▲▲

I. AS SNOW BEFORE A SUMMER SUN

THE COMING OF THE WHITE MAN:
THE PRETTY COLORED SNAKE

A Cherokee Story

In curiosity and friendship the Wampanoag tribe of
Massachusetts had welcomed the pilgrims aboard the
Mayflower to our shores. On Thanksgiving Day, 1970,
two hundred Indians from twenty-five tribes gathered
at Plymouth Rock to commemorate that occasion as a
national "Day of Mourning." A direct descendant of
that Wampanoag tribe declared this act of friendship
of his forefathers was their "greatest mistake." In
songs and stories, the Iroquois, Shawnee, Lakota, Anishinabe, and Arapaho voice this rueful hindsight.
"The Pretty Colored Snake" is a contemporary Cherokee version. (*Cherokee Stories,* by Reverend Watt
Spade and Willard Walker, Wesleyan University,
Conn., The Laboratory of Anthropology, 1966, pp.
22–3.)

A long time ago there was a famous hunter who used to go
all around hunting and always brought something good to
eat when he came home. One day he was going home with
some birds that he had shot, and he saw a little snake by the
side of the trail. It was a beautifully colored snake with all
pretty colors all over it, and it looked friendly too. The
hunter stopped and watched it for a while. He thought it
might be hungry, so he threw it one of his birds before he
went on home.

A few weeks later he was coming by the same place with some rabbits he had shot, and saw the snake again. It was still very beautiful and seemed friendly, but it had grown quite a bit. He threw it a rabbit and said "Hello" as he went on home.

Some time after that, the hunter saw the snake again. It had grown very big, but it was still friendly and seemed to be hungry. The hunter was taking some turkeys home with him, so he stopped and gave the snake a turkey gobbler.

Then, one time, the hunter was going home that way with two buck deer on his back. By this time, that pretty colored snake was very big and looked so hungry that the hunter felt sorry for him and gave him a whole buck to eat. When he got home, he heard that the people were going to have a stomp-dance. All the Nighthawks came, and that night they were going around the fire, dancing and singing the old songs, when the snake came and started going around too, outside of where the people were dancing. That snake was so big and long that he stretched all around the people and the people were penned up. The snake was covered all over with all pretty colors and he seemed friendly; but he looked hungry, too, and the people began to be afraid. They told some boys to get their bows and arrows and shoot the snake. Then the boys got their bows. They all shot together and they hit the snake all right. That snake was hurt. He thrashed his tail all around and killed a lot of the people.

They say that snake was just like the white man.

RESTORE TO US OUR COUNTRY

by Thayendanegea (General Joseph Brant)

The "League of Six Nations" of the Iroquois, one of the most formidable of tribal confederations, fought off invasions by the French, British, and Colonial armies. In pleading for peace, at the Council of 1793, the Mohawk orator and chief, Thayendanegea (Joseph Brant, 1742–1809), sounded a refrain that was to echo through American history. (*Aboriginal American Oratory*, by Louis Thomas Jones, Los Angeles, Cal., Southwest Museum, 1965, p. 28.)

Brothers: You have talked to us about concessions. It appears strange that you expect any from us, who have only been defending our just rights against your invasions. We want peace. Restore to us our country, and we shall be enemies no longer. . . .

Brothers: We desire you to consider that our only demand is the peaceable possession of a small part of our once great country. Look back and view the lands from whence we have been driven to this spot. We can retreat no farther, because the country behind hardly affords food for its present inhabitants; and we have therefore resolved to leave our bones in this small space, to which we now are consigned.

WILL WE LET OURSELVES BE DESTROYED?
by Tecumtha (Tecumseh)

"One of those uncommon geniuses [who] produced revolutions," wrote General William Henry Harrison of the Shawnee military leader Tecumtha (1768–1813). He sought to weld a tribal army from Florida to Ohio, to halt the white settlers at the Appalachians and drive them to the sea. If he had been successful, Harrison wrote, "he would perhaps be the founder of an Empire that would rival in glory that of Mexico or Peru." ("As Snow Before a Summer Sun," *Akwesasne*

Notes, Roosevelt, N.Y., Mohawk Nation, Vol. I, No. 5, May, 1969. "The Way . . . is for All the Redmen to Unite," *The Book of the Indians of North America,* by Samuel G. Drake, Boston, Mass., Antiquarian, 1836, pp. 121–2. "Let Our Affairs be Transacted by Warriors," *Aboriginal American Oratory,* pp. 85–6.)

As Snow Before a Summer Sun

Where today are the Pequot? Where are the Narragansett, the Mohican, the Pokanoket, and many other once powerful tribes of our people? They have vanished before the avarice and the oppression of the White Man, as snow before a summer sun.

Will we let ourselves be destroyed in our turn without a struggle, give up our homes, our country bequeathed to us by the Great Spirit, the graves of our dead, and everything that is dear and sacred to us?

I know you will cry with me, "Never! Never!"

"The Way . . . Is for All the Redmen to Unite"

I am a Shawnee. My forefathers were warriors. Their son is a warrior. From them I take only my existence, from my tribe I take nothing. I am the maker of my own fortune, and Oh! that I could make that of my Red people, and of my country, as great as the conceptions of my mind, when I think of the Spirit that rules the universe. I would not then come to Governor Harrison to ask him to tear up the treaty, and to obliterate the landmark, but I would say to him: "Sir, you have liberty to return to your own country."

The Being within, communing with past ages, tells me

that once, nor until lately, there was no Whiteman on this continent, that it then all belonged to the Redman, children of the same parents, placed on it by the Great Spirit that made them to keep it, to traverse it, to enjoy its productions, and to fill it with the same race, once a happy race; since made miserable by the White people, who are never contented but always encroaching.

The way, and the only way, to check and to stop this evil, is for all the Redmen to unite in claiming a common and equal right in the land, as it was at first and should be yet; for it was never divided, but belongs to all for the use of each. That no part has a right to sell, even to each other, much less to strangers—those who want all and will not do with less. The White people have no right to take the land from the Indians, because they had it first, it is theirs. They may sell, but all must join. Any sale not made by all, is not valid. The late sale is bad. It requires all to make a bargain for all. All Redmen have equal rights to the unoccupied land. The right to occupancy is as good in one place as in another. There cannot be two occupations in the same place. The first excludes all others. It is not so in hunting or traveling, for there the same ground will serve many, as they may follow each other all day, but the camp is stationary, and that is occupancy. It belongs to the first who sits down on his blanket or skins, which he has thrown upon the ground, and till he leaves it, no other has a right.

Let Our Affairs Be Transacted by Warriors

Brother! I wish you to listen to me well. As I think you do not clearly understand what I before said to you, I will explain it again.

Brother! Since the peace [of Greenville in 1795] was made, you have killed some of the Shawnees, Winnebagos, Delawares, and Miamis; and you have taken our lands from us; and I do not see how we can remain at peace with you, if you continue to do so . . . You take tribes aside, and advise them not to come into this measure [the confederacy]; and, until our design is accomplished, we do not wish to accept your invitation to go to see the president. . . .

Brother! You ought to know what you are doing with the Indians. . . . It is a very bad thing; and we do not like it. . . . We have endeavored to level all distinctions—to destroy village chiefs by whom all mischief is done. It is they who sell our lands to the Americans. Our object is to let our affairs be transacted by warriors. . . .

Brother! . . . If the land is not restored to us, you will see, when we return to our homes, how it will be settled. We shall have a great council, at which all the tribes will be present, when we shall show to those who sold, that they had no right to the claim they set up; and we will see what will be done with those chiefs.

IT IS HARD TO FIGHT AMONG BRETHREN FOR THE SAKE OF DOGS

by Pontiac

Like Tecumtha, "the great Pontiac" sought to unite the tribes against the invaders. A war chief of the Ottawas (1720–69), his tactics were said to have been responsible for the defeat of Lord Braddock in the French and Indian War. In the 1760's, he led a revolt of the Ohio tribes that captured eight of ten British forts on the Great Lakes, but his warriors were defeated by rival bands who sided with the British. And this led to his bitter speech. (*The Conspiracy of Pon-*

tiac and the Indian War After the Conquest of Canada, by Francis Parkman, Boston, Mass., Little Brown, 1898, pp. 292–3.)

My brothers, how long will you suffer this bad flesh to remain upon your lands? I have told you before, and I now tell you again, that when I took up the hatchet, it was for your good. This year the English must all perish throughout Canada. The Master of Life commands it; and you, who know him better than we, wish to oppose his will. Until now I have said nothing on this matter. I have not urged you to take part with us in the war. It would have been enough had you been content to sit quiet on your mats, looking on, while we were fighting for you. But you have not done so. You call yourselves our friends, and yet you assist the English with provisions, and go about as spies among our villages. This must not continue. You must be either wholly French or wholly English. If you are French, take up that war-belt, and lift the hatchet with us; but if you are English, then we declare war upon you. My brothers, I know this is a hard thing. We are all alike children of our Great Father the King of France, and it is hard to fight among brethren for the sake of dogs. But there is no choice. Look upon the belt, and let us hear your answer.

"HE DRANK THE BLOOD OF SOME WHITES": BLACK HAWK SPEAKS

The tribes did not unite. On the Mississippi River a new war chief arose to challenge the course of history: Black Hawk (1767–1838), of the Osakiwug (Sac) tribe, whose rich lands were taken from them by the Treaty of 1804. "I touched the goose quill to the treaty not knowing that, by that act, I consented to give away my village," Black Hawk said; his people were "forced into WAR by being DECEIVED!" After his death, Black Hawk's bones were stolen from his grave by whites and exhibited in the museum of the Historical Society in Burlington, Iowa. (*Akwesasne Notes*, Roosevelt, N.Y., Mohawk Nation, Vol. I, No. 6, June, 1969, p. 13.)

Black Hawk is an Indian. He has done nothing for which an Indian ought to be ashamed. He has fought for his countrymen, the squaws and papooses, against white men who came, year after year, to cheat them and take away their land. You know the cause of our making war. It is known to all white men. They ought to be ashamed of it. The white men despise the Indians, and drive them from their homes. But the Indians are not deceitful. The white men speak bad of the Indian, and look at him spitefully. But the Indian does not tell lies; Indians do not steal.

An Indian who is as bad as the white men could not live in our nation; he would be put to death, and eat up by the wolves. The white men are bad school-masters; they carry false looks, and deal in false actions; they smile in the face of the poor Indian to cheat him; they shake them by the hand to gain their confidence, to make them drunk, to deceive them, and ruin our wives. We told them to let us alone; but they followed on and beset our paths, and they coiled themselves among us like the snake. They poisoned us by their touch. We were not safe. We lived in danger. We were becoming like them, hypocrites and liars, adulterers, lazy drones, all talkers, and no workers.

We looked up to the Great Spirit. We went to our great father. We were encouraged. His great council gave us fair words and big promises, but we got no satisfaction. Things were growing worse. There were no deer in the forest. The oppossum and beaver were fled; the springs were drying up, and our squaws and papooses without victuals to keep them from starving; we called a great council and built a large fire. The spirit of our fathers arose and spoke to us to avenge our wrongs or die. . . . We set up the war-whoop, and dug up the tomahawk; our knives were ready, and the heart of Black Hawk swelled high in his bosom when he led his warriors to battle. He is satisfied. He will go to the world of spirits contented. He has done his duty. His father will meet him there, and commend him.

Black Hawk is a true Indian, and disdains to cry like a woman. He feels for his wife, his children, and friends. But he does not care for himself. He cares for his nation and the Indians. They will suffer. He laments their fate. The white men do not scalp the head; but they do worse—they poison the heart, it is not pure with them. His countrymen will not be scalped, but they will, in a few years, become like the white men, so that you can't trust them, and there must be, as in the white settlements, nearly as many officers as men, to take care of them and keep them in order.

Farewell, my nation. Black Hawk tried to save you, and avenge your wrongs. He drank the blood of some whites. He has been taken prisoner, and his plans are stopped. He can do no more. He is near his end. His sun is setting, and he will rise no more. Farewell to Black Hawk.

OUR NEW HOME WILL BE BEYOND A GREAT RIVER

by Keokuk

Old Keokuk, unlike Black Hawk, was an Osakiwug chief who thought it hopeless to continue the fight. In 1821, General William Clark, the Governor of the Missouri Territory, offered Keokuk (1780–1848) several thousand dollars for his tribe, and a few hundred dollars' worth of velvet coats, plumes, and silk handkerchiefs for himself, if he would convince his people to abandon their village. "I looked upon him as a coward," Black Hawk said; but Keokuk, a troubled old man with frightened eyes, believed he was saving his people from certain defeat. (*Aboriginal American Oratory*, p. 96.)

Brother! My people and myself have come to shake hands with you. The time for us to go has come. We do not feel glad to leave this country which we have lived in so long.

The many moons and sunny days we have lived here will long be remembered by us. The Great Spirit has smiled upon us and made us glad. But we have agreed to go.

We go to a country we know but little of. Our new home will be beyond a great river on the way to the setting sun. We will build our wigwams there in another land where we hope the Great Spirit will smile upon us, as he has here.

The men we leave here in possession of these lands cannot say Keokuk and his people have ever taken up the tomahawk . . . against them. We have always been for peace with you, and you have been kind to us. In peace we bid you goodbye. May the Great Spirit smile upon you in this land, and upon us in the new land to which we go. We will think of you and you must think of us. If you come to see us, we will divide our supply of venison with you and we will gladly welcome you.

THOSE WHO MADE WAR AGAINST THE WHITE MAN ALWAYS FAILED . . .

by Aleek-chea-ahoosh (Plenty-Coups)

Some tribes were used by the whites; some tribes *used* the whites. In Montana, the Chief of the Absarokees (Crow), known as Aleek-chea-ahoosh, or Plenty-Coups (1848–1932), was a master of Machiavellian warfare. "All tribes were against us," Plenty-Coups said. He allied his tribe with the U.S. Army to defeat the Lakota (Sioux), Striped-Feathered-Arrows (Cheyenne) and Tattooed-Breasts (Arapaho). His diplomatic achievement earned him the respect of his tribe, but less than respect among the neighboring tribes. (*Plenty-Coups, Chief of the Crows*, by Frank B. Linderman, Omaha, Neb., University of Nebraska Press, 1962, pp. 77–8, 153–4, 227–8 and 307–8.)

I do not know if there have been other tribes who fought with the white men and never against them, as we have done. Listening, as the chickadee listens, we saw that those who made war against the white men always failed in the end and lost their lands. Look at the Striped-Feathered-Arrows (Cheyenne). Most of them are living where they hate the ground that holds their lodges. They cannot look at the mountains as I can or drink good water as I do every day. Instead of making a treaty with the white men and by it holding their country which they loved, they fought. Ah!

how those warriors fought! And lost all, taking whatever the white man would give. And when the hearts of the givers are filled with hate their gifts are small.

The Cheyenne, and the Sioux who fare a little better, have always been our enemies, but I am sorry for them today. I have fought hard against them in war, with the white man more than once, and often with my own tribe before the white man came. But when I fought with the white man against them it was not because I loved him or because I hated the Sioux and Cheyenne, but because I saw that this was the only way we could keep our lands. Look at our country! It was chosen by my people out of the heart of the most beautiful land on all the world, because we were wise. And it was my dream that taught us the way.

I was a chief when I was twenty-eight and well remember that when white men found gold in the Black Hills the Sioux and Cheyenne made war on them. The Crows were wiser. We knew the white men were strong, without number in their own country, and that there was no good in fighting them; so that when other tribes wished us to fight them we refused. Our leading chiefs saw that to help the white men fight their enemies and ours would make them our friends. We had always fought the three tribes, Sioux, Cheyenne, and Arapaho, anyway, and might as well do so now. The complete destruction of our old enemies would please us. Our decision was reached, not because we loved the white man who was already crowding other tribes into our country, or because we hated the Sioux, Cheyenne, and Arapaho, but because we plainly saw that this course was the only one which might save our beautiful country for us. When I think back my heart sings because we acted as we did. It was the only way open to us.

By the time I was forty, I could see that our country was changing fast, and that these changes were causing us to live very differently. Anybody could now see that soon there would be no buffalo on the plains, and everybody was wondering how we could live after they were gone. . . . We made up our minds to be friendly with them, in spite of all the changes they were bringing. But we found this difficult, because the white men too often promised to do one thing and then, when they acted at all, did another.

They spoke very loudly when they said their laws were made for everybody; but we soon learned that although they expected us to keep them, they thought nothing of breaking them themselves. They told us not to drink whiskey, yet they made it themselves and traded it to us for furs and robes until both were nearly gone. Their Wise Ones said we might have their religion, but when we tried to understand it we found that there were too many kinds of religion among white men for us to understand, and that scarcely any two white men agreed which was the right one to learn. This bothered us a good deal until we saw that the white man did not take his religion any more seriously than he did his laws, and that he kept both of them just behind him, like Helpers, to use when they might do him good in his dealings with strangers. These were not our ways. We kept the laws we made and lived our religion. We have never been able to understand the white man, who fools nobody but himself. . . .

All my life I have tried to learn as the chickadee learns, by listening—profiting by the mistakes of others, that I might help my people. I hear the white men say there will be no more war. But this cannot be true. There will be other wars. Men have not changed, and whenever they quarrel they will fight, as they have always done. We love our country because it is beautiful, because we were born here. Strangers will covet it and some day try to possess it, as surely as the sun will come tomorrow. Then there must be war, unless we have grown to be cowards without love in our hearts for our native land. And whenever war comes between this country and another your people will find my people pointing their guns with yours. My heart sings with pride when I think of the fighting my people, the red men of all tribes, did in this last great war; and if ever the hands of my own people hold the rope that keeps this country's flag high in the air, it will never come down while an Absarokee warrior lives.

Remember this, Sign-talker, and help my people keep their lands. Help them to hold forever the Pryor and Big-horn mountains. They love them as I do and deserve to have them for the help they have given the white man, who now owns all.

I am old. I am not graceful. My bones are heavy, and my feet are large. But I know justice and have tried all my life to be just, even to those who have taken away our old life that was so good. My whole thought is of my people. I want them to be healthy, to become again the race they have been. I want them to learn all they can from the white man, because he is here to stay, and they must live with him forever.

IT IS A GOOD DAY TO DIE!

"It is a good day to die!" was the Lakota (Sioux) war cry. The "Uprising of 1862" in Minnesota was fought by Lakota bands to protest the Treaty of Traverse des Sioux, by which the U.S. government acquired, but never paid for, 24,000,000 acres of tribal land. Chief Shakopee delivered his prophetic eulogy for his warriors before this battle. (*North Star Country*, by Meridel Le Seuer, New York, Book Find Club, 1945, p. 88.)

And a few years later, at the Council of Fort Laramie, Red Cloud (1833–1909), the leader of the Oglala band, the Bad Faces, echoed the strident cry for war. (*Aborginal American Oratory*, p. 102.)

You Are Like Dogs in the Hot Moon

by Chief Shakopee

You are like dogs in the hot moon, when they go mad and snap and bite. We are only a little herd of buffalo left scattered. The great herds that once covered the prairies are no more.

The white men are like locusts when they fly so thick that the whole sky is like a snowstorm. You may kill one, two, ten; yes, as many as the leaves in the forest yonder, and their brothers will not miss them. Count your fingers all day long and white men with guns in their hands will come faster than you can count. You are fools, you die like rabbits when the hungry wolves hunt them in the hard moon.

I am no coward. I shall die with you.

Dakotas, I Am for War!

by Red Cloud

Hear ye, Dakotas! When the Great Father at Washington sent us his chief soldier to ask for a path through our hunting grounds, a way for his iron road to the mountains and the western sea, we were told that they wished merely to pass through our country, not to tarry among us, but to seek for gold in the far west. Our old chiefs thought to show their friendship and good will, when they allowed this dangerous snake in our midst. . . .

Yet, before the ashes of the council fire were cold, the Great Father is building his forts among us. You have heard the sound of the white soldier's ax upon the Little Piney. His presence here is an insult and a threat. It is an insult to the spirits of our ancestors. Are we then to give up their sacred graves to be plowed for corn? Dakotas, I am for war!

THE DAY BEFORE THE BATTLE ON THE LITTLE BIG HORN
by Lloyd Winter Chaser

Histories of the "Indian Wars," more accurately "Wars Against the Indians," have been told most often from the whites' viewpoint. None have been told more often, and more inaccurately, than the stories of the Battle of the Little Big Horn, in 1876—the defeat of Custer. For generations the Indians would not tell what happened, for fear of reprisals. Now, the Indians' story is beginning to be heard, as in "The Day Before The Battle," by an old Dakota historian, Lloyd Winter Chaser, of the Rosebud Reservation. (*Rosebud Sioux Herald*, Rosebud, S.D., Oct. 20, 1969, p. 2.)

It was a hot summer day when three boys, ages 17 to 19, were out miles away from the camp. They were practicing on their bows and arrows while hunting small game.

They climbed up to the top of a hill to rest where there was a little breeze.

While they were resting, around noon, they saw something off in the distance which looked like a herd of buffalo, moving towards the camp.

This made the boys very happy because when they get

home they will tell the hunters, and they will have meat in the teepees.

One of the boys had binoculars so they looked through them to make sure they were buffalos. But what they saw through the binoculars were not buffalos.

They saw something shine once in a while among that moving herd. One of the boys said, "I'm sure buffalos don't carry looking glass."

All of a sudden it dawned on them that it could be the cavalry moving, but where?

One of the boys said: "Let's go and see what that moving herd was, if it were buffalo tracks or horse tracks."

When they reached the place they were surprised to see horse tracks, not buffalo, so they knew right away that it was a cavalry moving towards the Indians' encampment.

One of the boys jokingly said: "I thought we were going to have meat, but now it will be horses and scalps."

It was towards evening when the boys got back to camp. The Indians were having dances or pow wows in several different places. Instead of going back to their teepees, they took part in the dancing, going from one dance to another.

Chasing young squaws, they forgot how late it was and of the cavalry moving towards their camp.

In the Indian way, when a boy is 20 years old, the older Indians consider him as a little child. In the modern way, we might call them "still in diapers" or "wet behind the ears."

The three boys were trying to court one older squaw, about in her 30's, a teenager in those days.

This squaw said: "Tukee le wakanhe ja ska omayutantan" or "My, he's such a little boy, but going too fast."

Finally they got tired of chasing and one of them said: "Let's not go home, but stay here under this tree and rest."

They were awakened by women and children in the river swimming and washing clothes, and just having a good time, never thinking of what was to take place there in just a few hours.

It was really peaceful for the Indians. The nature, which was all the Indians live with, was kind to them that peaceful morning.

OUR PEOPLE ARE BLINDLY DECEIVED
by Sitting Bull

Pretty Bird, you came and pitied me;
You wished my people to live.
Bird people, I am your brother.

Sitting Bull was a wise man of the Hunkpapa band of Teton Lakota. As he was a poet and prophet, it was his vision that prophesied the defeat of General Custer, when the gold seekers invaded the sacred Black Hills of the Lakotas. And when the Lakota were confined to reservations and massacred at Wounded Knee, Sitting Bull wrote their epitaph: "No chance for me to live. Mother mourn for me." (*Great Plains Observer*, Jan., 1969, p. 14.)

Friends and Relatives: Our minds are again disturbed by the Great Father's representatives, the Indian Agent, the squaw-men, the mixed-bloods, the interpreters, and the favorite-ration-chiefs. What is it they want of us at this time? They want us to give up another chunk of our tribal land. This is not the first time nor the last time. They will try to gain possession of the last piece of ground we possess. They are again telling us what they intend to do if we agree to their wishes. Have we ever set a price on our land and received such a value? No, we never did. What we got under the former treaties were promises of all sorts. They promised how we are going to live peaceably on the land we still own and how they are going to show us the new ways of living, even told us how we can go to heaven when we die, but all that we realized out of the agreements with the Great Father was, we are dying off in expectation of getting things promised us.

One thing I wish to state at this time is, something tells me that the Great Father's representatives have again brought with them a well-worded paper, containing just what they want but ignoring our wishes in the matter. It is this that they are attempting to drive us to. Our people are blindly deceived. Some are in favor of the proposition, but we who realize that our children and grandchildren may live a little longer must necessarily look ahead and flatly reject the proposition. I, for one, am bitterly opposed to it. The Great Father has proven himself an *unktomi* [trickster] in our past dealings.

When the white people invaded our Black Hills country our treaty agreements were still in force but the Great Father ignored it—pretending to keep out the intruders through military force, and at last failing to keep them out they had to let them come in and take possession of our best part of our tribal possession. Yet the Great Father maintains a very large standing army that can stop anything.

Therefore, I do not wish to consider any proposition to cede any portion of our tribal holdings to the Great Father. If I agree to dispose of any part of our land to the white people I would feel guilty of taking food away from our children's mouths, and I do not wish to be that mean. There are things they tell us sound good to hear, but when they have accomplished their purpose they will go home and will not try to fulfill our agreements with them.

My friends and relatives, let us stand as one family as we did before the white people led us astray.

THE SURRENDER OF GERONIMO:
"I WAS LIVING QUIETLY AND CONTENTED,
DOING AND THINKING OF NO HARM . . ."

Geronimo's "Surrender Speech" has been called "the first Indian put-on." A medicine man of the Bedonkohes band of Chiricahua Apaches (1834–1909), he led his band of 130 men, women, and children into the mountains, where for 18 months they eluded 5,000 U.S. Army troops and vigilantes. In later years, his captor, General George F. Crook, said: "I venture to prophesy that as time passes . . . we will decide he was one of the greatest 'Americans' that ever lived." (*Report of Captain John G. Bourke, 3rd Cavalry, to Lt. Gen. P. H. Sheridan, of a Conference held on March 25th and 27th, 1886, at Canon de Los Embudos, Arizona, U.S. Army Archives.*)

GERONIMO: I want to talk first of the causes which led me to leave the reservation. I was living quietly and contented, doing and thinking of no harm, while at the Sierra Blanca. I don't know what harm I did . . . I was living peaceably with my family, having plenty to eat, sleeping well, taking care of my people, and perfectly contented. I don't know where those bad stories came from. There we were doing well and my people well. I was behaving well. I hadn't killed a horse or man, American or Indian. I don't know what was the matter with the people in charge of us. They knew this to be so, and yet they said I was a bad man and the worst man there, but what harm had I done? I was liv-

ing peaceably and well, but I did not leave on my own
accord.

Some time before I left an Indian named Wodiskay had a
talk with me. He said, "They are going to arrest you," but I
paid no attention to him, knowing that I had done no
wrong; and the wife of Mangus, "Huera," told me that they
were going to seize me and put me and Mangus in the
guard-house, and I learned from the American and Apache
soldiers, from Chato, and Mickey Free, that the Americans
were going to arrest me and hang me, and so I left.

I want to know now who it was ordered me to be arrested. I was praying to the light and to the darkness, to
God and to the sun, to let me live quietly there with my
family. I don't know what the reason was that people should
speak badly of me. I don't want to be blamed. The fault was
not mine.

Now I am going to tell you something else. The Earth-
Mother is listening to me and I hope that all may be so ar-
ranged that from now on there shall be no trouble and that
we shall always have peace. Whenever we see you coming
to where we are, we think that it is God—you must come always with God. From this time on I do not want that anything shall be told you about me even in joke. Whenever I
have broken out, it has always been on account of bad talk.
From this time on I hope that people will tell me nothing
but the truth.

What is the matter that you don't speak to me? It would
be better if you would speak to me and look with a pleasant
face. It would make better feeling. I would be glad if you
did. I'd be better satisfied if you would talk to me once in a
while. Why don't you look at me and smile at me? I am the
same man; I have the same feet, legs, and hands, and the
sun looks down on me a complete man. I want you to look
and smile at me.

I am a complete man. Nothing has gone from my body. From here on I want to live at peace.

I never do wrong without a cause. Every day I am thinking, how am I to talk to you to make you believe what I say; and, I think, too, that you are thinking of what you are to say to me. There is one God looking down on us all. We are all children of the one God. God is listening to me. The sun, the darkness, the winds, are all listening to what we now say.

GENERAL CROOK: I have heard what you have said. . . . If that was a fact, that you left the reservation for that reason, why did you kill innocent people, sneaking all over the country to do it? What did those innocent people do to you that you should kill them, steal their horses, and slip around in the rocks like coyotes?

GERONIMO: We did not know what we had done. . . .

GENERAL CROOK: That's all bosh. . . .

GERONIMO: I am a man of my word. I am telling the truth and why I left the reservation.

GENERAL CROOK: You told me the same thing in the Sierra Madre, but you lied.

GERONIMO: Then how do you want me to talk to you? I have but one mouth. I can't talk with my ears.

GENERAL CROOK: Your mouth talks too many ways.

GERONIMO: If you think I am not telling the truth, then I don't think you came down here in good faith.

[*Later*]

GERONIMO: Two or three words are enough. I have little to say. I surrender myself to you. (*Shakes hands with General Crook*) We are all comrades, all one family, all one band. What the others say I say also. I give myself up to you. Do with me what you please. I surrender. Once I moved like the wind. Now I surrender to you, and that is all.

(*Shakes hands with General Crook*) . . . My heart is yours, and I hope yours will be mine. (*Shakes hands*) Now I feel like your brother. . . . (*Shakes hands*) I have no lies in my heart. Whatever you tell me is true. I hope the day may come when my word shall be as strong with you as yours is with me. . . . Now I want to let Alchisay and Ka-e-te-na speak a few words. . . .

KA-E-TE-NA: Let Alchisay speak for me. I have a sore throat.

ALCHISAY: I am talking now for the Chiricahua. . . . [We] are all the same people. All one family with me. Just like when you kill a deer, all its parts are of one body. So with the Chiricahua. . . . A hen has many chickens. She goes, the chickens follow. So are you going over to Apache Pass and we are coming along behind you. Now, we want to travel along the open road and drink the waters of the Americans, and not hide in the mountains. We want to live without danger and discomfort.

"YOUR PEOPLE HAVE DESTROYED MY NATION"

by Red Eagle

Once the Creeks were among the largest tribes in the South, thought to number 20,000 in 1800. The slaughter of the Creeks by the troops of General Andrew Jackson was one of the bloodiest massacres in Indian history. In a few months, the U.S. Army killed 2,000 men, women, and children, burned their villages and fields, and then at Horseshoe Bend, on the Tallapoosa River, killed another 5,000 to 7,000. Red Eagle, a half-breed known also as William Weatherford, is still blamed by some Creeks for this debacle. (*Aboriginal American Oratory*, p. 66.)

I am in your power; do with me as you please. I am a soldier. I have done the white people all the harm I could; I have fought them, and fought them bravely. If I had an army, I would yet fight and contend to the last; but I have none; my people are all gone. I can do no more than weep over the misfortunes of my nation. Once I could animate my warriors to battle; but I cannot animate the dead. My warriors can no longer hear my voice: their bones are at *Talladega, Tallushatches, Emuckfaw,* and *Tohopeka.* I have not surrendered myself thoughtlessly. While there were chances of success I never left my post, nor supplicated peace; but my people are now gone, and I ask it for my nation and for myself. On the miseries and misfortunes brought on my country, I look back with deepest sorrow, and I wish to avert still greater calamities. If I had been left to contend with the Georgia army alone, I would have raised my corn on one bank of the river and fought them on the other; but your people have destroyed my nation. You are a brave man; I rely on your generosity. You will exact no terms of a conquered people, but such as they should accede to: whatever they may be, it would be madness and folly to oppose. If they are opposed, you will find me among the sternest enforcers of obedience. Those who would still hold out can only be influenced by a mean spirit of revenge; and to this they must not and shall not sacrifice the last remnant of their country.

"I WILL FIGHT NO MORE FOREVER"

by Highn'moot Tooyalakekt (Chief Joseph)

Chief Joseph was not his name. He was known as
Highn'moot Tooyalakekt—the "Thunder Going to the
High Mountains." In 1877, after "White men cheated,
bullied, and murdered Nez Perce," writes Alvin Jose-
phy in *The Patriot Chiefs*, Highn'moot Tooyalakekt led
his people out of Oregon on one of the great military
retreats in history, 1,500 miles to Canada. Like his retreat, his surrender speech is a classic of tribal pride
and resolve. (*The Writing on the Wall*, edited by Walter Lowenfels, New York, Doubleday and Company,
1969, p. 121.)

I am tired of fighting. Our chiefs are killed. Looking Glass is
dead. Toohulsote is dead. The old men are all dead. It is the
young men who say no and yes. He who led the young men
is dead. It is cold and we have no blankets. The little children are freezing to death. My people, some of them, have
run away to the hills and have no blankets, no food. No one
knows where they are—perhaps they are freezing to death.
I want to have time to look for my children and see how
many of them I can find. Maybe I shall find them among the
dead. Hear me, my chiefs, I am tired. My heart is sad and
sick. From where the sun now stands I will fight no more
forever.

"DEAD, DID I SAY? THERE IS NO DEATH . . ."

by Chief Seathe (Seattle)

It was but a few years after the defeat of the tribes and the speeches of surrender that a new prophecy arose of Indian rebirth. Seathe (Seattle), a chief of the small Duwamish tribe on Puget Sound, in Washington Territory, forecast that prophecy in signing the Treaty of Port Elliot, in 1855. In giving up his lands in return for the right to fish in peace, the old chief warned the white man that he was doomed to eternal unrest, haunted by "the invisible dead of my tribe." (*Aboriginal American Oratory*, p. 99.)

Yonder sky that has wept tears of compassion on our fathers for centuries untold, and which, to us, looks eternal, may change. Today is fair, tomorrow it may be overcast with clouds. My words are like the stars that never change. What Seattle says, the great chief Washington can rely upon, with as much certainty as our paleface brothers can rely upon the return of the seasons.

The son of the White Chief says that his father sends us greetings of friendship and good will. This is kind, for we know he has little need of our friendship in return, because his people are many. They are like the grass that covers the vast prairies. My people are few, and resemble the scattering trees of a storm-swept plain. . . .

There was a time when our people covered the whole land as the waves of the wind-ruffled sea cover its shell-paved floor. But that time has long since passed away with the greatness of tribes now almost forgotten. I will not mourn over our untimely decay, nor reproach my paleface brothers with hastening it. . . .

Your religion was written on tablets of stone, by the iron

finger of your God, lest you forget it. The red men could never remember it or comprehend it. Our religion is the traditions of our ancestors, the dreams of our old men, given them by the Great Spirit, and the visions of our sachems, and is written in the hearts of our people. . . .

Every part of this country is sacred to my people. Every hillside, every valley, every plain and grove has been hallowed by some fond memory or some sad experience of my tribe. Even the rocks which seem to lie dumb as they swelter in the sun . . . thrill with memories of past events connected with the fate of my people. . . .

The braves, fond mothers, glad-hearted maidens, and even little children, who lived here . . . still love these solitudes. Their deep fastnesses at eventide grow shadowy with the presence of dusty spirits. When the last red man shall have perished from the earth and his memory among the white men shall have become a myth, these shores shall swarm with the invisible dead of my tribe. . . .

At night when the streets of your cities and villages shall be silent, and you think them deserted, they will throng with the returning hosts that once filled and still love this beautiful land.

The white man will never be alone. Let him be just and deal kindly with my people, for the dead are not altogether powerless. Dead, did I say? There is no death, only a change of worlds.

II. SONGS OF THE PEOPLE

SONGS OF THE PEOPLE (ANISHINABE NAGAMON)

by Gerald Vizenor

In the past, the wisdom and tales and philosophy of the tribes was most often translated and interpreted by anthropologists. They were often technically accurate, but just as often they lost the religious power and aesthetic beauty of the originals. A new generation of tribal scholars has arisen, who are re-translating and re-interpreting the literature of their peoples. One of these is Gerald Vizenor, an Anishinabe of the White Earth Reservation, a poet, newspaper man, and mystic, who renders the nuances and shadows of the songs of the Anishinabe (Chippewa). ("Introduction," in *Anishinabe Nagamon*, by Gerald Vizenor, Minn., Nodin Press, 1965, pp. 9–17.)

The sacred *migis* shell of the *Anishinabe* spirit arose from the eastern sea and moved along the inland waters guiding *the people* through the sleeping sun of the woodland to *bawitig*—the long rapids in the river.

The *Anishinabe*—the *original people* of the woodland—believe they were given wisdom and life color from the sun reflecting on the sacred shell during this long migration. Five hundred years ago, the *migis* shell appeared in the sun for the last time at *Moningwanekaning* in *Anishinabe kitchigami*—the great sea of the *Anishinabe*.

The people measured living through time in the circles on the sun and moon and human heart. Trailing the summer shores of *kitchigami* to the hardwoods and swamps, drawing *sisibakwat,* and gathering *manomin,* the *Anishinabe* returned each winter to *Moningwanekaning*—Madeline Island in Lake Superior—and told stories of the summer heart.

In the seventeenth century, voyagers and the first missionaries of the old world established a Christian fur trading post on *Moningwanekaning* near the sacred community of *the people.* While showing the new world discoverers how to endure the long woodland winters, only half of the *Anishinabe* survived the first pestilence of the white man—a severe smallpox epidemic.

Fulgurant missionaries latinized the woodland dead and thundered through the Epistles that *the people* were only children learning the hymns of a new civilization. The hymns were peddled like military secrets to the nervy voyagers who learned the language and life style of the woodland and enmeshed *the people* in the predatory economics of peltry.

The expanding interests of the fur trade—spurred by the old world bourgeois demand for felt hats—drew *the people* to other fur trading posts with beaver peltry in exchange for firearms and diluted intoxicants.

moving forward and back
from the woodland to the prairie
Dakota women
weeping
as they gather
their wounded men
the sound of their weeping
comes back to us

With rifles the *Anishinabe* easily defeated the woodland *Dakota* and drove them from the rich wild rice lands in northern Minnesota.

The fur trade interposed an economic anomaly between the intuitive rhythm of woodland life and the equipoise of the *Anishinabe* spirit. While *the people* were reluming the human unity of tribal life, thousands of sainted white settlers procured the land with new laws and enslaved the *Anishinabe* in the fury of discovery.

> honoring your brave men
> like them
> believing in myself

The rhythm of the land was broken by the marching cadence of Christian patriotism. *Anishinabe* orators of the *mang odem*, legions of the *makwa odem*, and *the people* of the *amik odem*, were colonized and mythologized and alienated from their woodland life and religion while the voices of the conquerors rang with freedom.

> brave warriors
> where have you gone
> *ho kwi ho ho*

The *Anishinabe* did not have a written history. The past was a visual memory and oratorical gesture of dreams plaiting an endless woodland identity between the conscious and unconscious worlds of *the people*.

I am a bird . . . if you wish to know me you must seek me in the clouds . . . the Anishinabe orator *Keeshkemun* told the *jaganash* military officers who had asked him to explain his position in the new world territorial wars. *Keeshkemun* responded to the question with a personal dream song.

The song poems of the *Anishinabe* are intuitive lyrical images of woodland life.

> the first to come
> epithet among the birds
> bringing the rain
> crow is my name

The *Anishinabe* hears music not only in the human voice, but in the sounds of animals and trees and ice cracking on the lakes. *The people* are surrounded by life. They are not alone.

> the wind
> only
> fearing him

Anishinabemowin is a language of verbal forms and word images. The spoken feeling of the language is a moving image of tribal woodland life: *nibi*—water, *mang*—loon, *makwa*—bear, *amik*—beaver, kingfishers at dusk, the owls at night, and maple syrup in the snow.

The language is euphonious: *Anishinabe nagamon*—songs of the people, *pipigwan*—flute, *manomin*—wild rice, *gimi-wan*—rain, *sibi*—river, *memengwa*—butterfly, *nibawin*—sleeping, *sisibakwat*—maple sugar, *ishkote*—fire, *papakine*—grasshopper, *wawatessi*—firefly.

And the words are descriptive: *missanwi*—snow falling from the branches, *kijiga*—maple sap is running fast from the trees, *onabani gisiss*—the month of the moon on the crust of the snow, *sagashka*—grass begins to grow, *papakine magad ishkote*—crackling fire.

The *Anishinabe* drew pictures of ideas and presentient

dreams. The song pictures of the *midewiwin*—the sacred
life of *the people*—were incised on the soft inner bark of the
birch. These scrolls of pictomyths and sacred songs are
taught and understood only by members of the *midewiwin*
who believe that music and the knowledge and use of herbal
medicine prolong life.

Anishinabe song poetry is a symphony of cosmic rhythms
and tribal instincts, memories and dream songs, expressing
the contrasts of life and death, day and night, man and
woman, courage and fear.

> my feathers
> sailing
> on the breeze

The song words of the woodland poet are like the feathers
of birds lifting one by one on the wind—the shadows of
death escaping through avian dreams.

> the clear sky
> loves to hear me sing

The presentient dreams of the *Anishinabe* are expressed
in songs like the spontaneous rhythm of breathing.

> overhanging clouds
> echoing my words
> with a pleasing sound

The people do not fear silence and space. In the past the
Anishinabe knew self-reverence and disciplined himself
against the excesses of human desires and possessions. Visions were imperfect and dreams were the songs of history.

> across the earth
> everywhere
> making my voice heard

The song poems of the *Anishinabe* are songs of individual freedom. The dreams are not forgotten. The woodland voice of *the people* may still be heard wavering over the mourning bell of decadent promises for peace.

A WORD HAS POWER

by N. Scott Momaday

> In 1970, the thousand-year-old literatures of the tribes were nationally recognized by the awarding of the Pulitzer Prize to the Kiowa writer, N. Scott Momaday, for his novel *House Made of Dawn* (New York, Harper & Row). Momaday seeks to place tribal literature in historical perspective in *The Way to Rainy Mountain* by portraying it as three truths: first, that of tribal "legend"; second, that of philosophical meaning; and, third, that of personal experience. (*The Way to Rainy Mountain*, by N. Scott Momaday, Albuquerque, N. Mex., University of New Mexico Press, 1969, pp. 32–3.)

Now, each of the twins had a ring, and the grandmother spider told them never to throw the rings into the sky. But, one day, they threw them up into the high wind. The rings rolled over a hill and the twins ran after them. They ran beyond the top of the hill and fell down into the mouth of a cave. There lived a giant and his wife. The giant had killed a lot of people in the past by building fires and filling the cave with smoke, so that the people could not breathe. Then the twins remembered something that the grandmother spider had told them: "If ever you get caught in the cave, say to yourselves the word *thain-mom*, 'above my eyes.'" When the giant began to set fires around, the twins repeated the word *thain-mom* over and over to themselves, and the smoke remained above their eyes. When the giant had made three great clouds of smoke, his wife saw that the twins sat without coughing or crying and she became frightened. "Let them go," she said, "or something bad will happen to us." The twins took up their rings and returned to the grandmother spider. She was glad to see them.

⁞   ⁞   ⁞

A WORD HAS POWER IN AND OF ITSELF. IT COMES FROM NOTHING INTO SOUND AND MEANING; IT GIVES ORIGIN TO ALL THINGS. BY MEANS OF WORDS CAN A MAN DEAL WITH THE WORLD ON EQUAL TERMS. AND THE WORD IS SACRED. A MAN'S NAME IS HIS OWN; HE CAN KEEP IT OR GIVE IT AWAY AS HE LIKES. UNTIL RECENT TIMES, THE KIOWAS WOULD NOT SPEAK THE NAME OF A DEAD MAN. TO DO SO WOULD HAVE BEEN DISRESPECTFUL AND DISHONEST. THE DEAD TAKE THEIR NAMES WITH THEM OUT OF THE WORLD.

⁞   ⁞   ⁞

When Aho saw or heard or thought of something bad, she said the word zei-dl-bei, *"frightful." It was the one word with which she confronted evil and the incomprehensible. I liked her to say it, for she screwed up her face in a wonderful look of displeasure and clicked her tongue. It was not an exclamation so much, I think, as it was a warding-off, an exertion of language upon ignorance and disorder.*

THE MYSTERIOUS BIRD
AND THE LAND OF THE DEATH

by Jaime de Angulo

> If a word has a reality, or power, in and of itself in
> tribal literature, as N. Scott Momaday writes, then a
> feather, or a color, has meaning in and of itself in tribal
> drama or ritual, writes Jaime de Angulo. Having lived
> much of his life among the California tribes about
> whom he writes, De Angulo eschews anthropological
> methodology to evoke the reality of the people as they
> saw it and experienced it. (*Indian Tales*, by Jaime de
> Angulo, New York, Hill and Wang, 1953, pp. 141–6.)

At Katimin they lived long ago, two very good flint-carriers.
And at Mahiniva each one had a sweetheart. Then both
men got sick, and both of them died. The girls grieved very
much.

Near their home a very old woman had died not long before. They used to carry her around on a stretcher. All at
once, she said, "Carry me outside." When they had put her
down outside, she said, "Look over there across. They are
dancing the Deer Dance, the dancers are dancing along the
ridge." Then a fog rose where she had been lying and it
floated across the river and up the side of the mountain.
That old woman had been world-maker ten times.

Every morning early, the two girls got out to gather
wood. They go to Top-of-the-Bank. That is the place where
they stand, the trimmed trees of their lovers, the memorial
trees trimmed of all branches except two, pointing to east
and west. The girls go there and cry when they look at the
trimmed trees.

Summer came at last.

One morning early, the girls were there, crying, at the

place where they always go. While they were looking at
their trimmed trees, all at once someone spoke to them. It
was the Bird, the mysterious Bird who lives with his mate
near the top of Sugar Loaf Hill. Each year he takes their
brood to the Land of the Dead and leaves them there.

"Hey! are you feeling sad about your lovers?" he asked.

"Yes, yes!"

Then he said, "I had better take you there. I am the only
one who goes there where they are now."

And they said, "All right!"

"You can only look at them. They won't come back. But I
feel sorry for you whenever I see you crying here." And
then he said, "In ten days you must be ready, then you must
come early in the morning to Rock Hill Ridge. That is the
time I take my children to the Land of the Dead, and I will
take you, too."

And then, at last, they counted that ten days had passed.
It was the time he had told them to be ready. While it was
still dark, the Bird's children began calling. When the girls
heard them, they too set out at once. Then they sat down at
Rock Hill Ridge. They had not been waiting long when they
heard the Bird's children calling, and saw them flying past
overhead.

Then the Bird called down to them, "You keep traveling
along below us."

So they climbed the ridge. And finally, at the top, they
could look far into the distance and see that it was one long
ridge, the same as that on which they were walking. And,
above them, the Bird's children were traveling along.

At last they had come a long way. Then, it seemed as
though they were going down. The Bird's children said,
"We're nearly there." They looked and saw only side hills of
brush all around, elderbrush—it was the only kind there
was. And when they reached the foot they found a river

flowing. And there was also a house. The roof of the house looked grey from all the birds that perched on it.

But no one looked at the girls. Close to the eaves of the house they stood, and the birds who had come with them perched on the roof.

He said to them, the Bird, "Don't go around. Don't go looking around."

But they looked around. There were all kinds of gambling games going on around them. Then at dusk the people made a big fire outside. All around it was swept clear.

Then the one who had brought them, that one said, "This is the only way you can see your lovers. They are going to dance the Deer Dance. Go and stand there, one at each end of the line. There they will be carrying the flints, your lovers." And at both ends of the line they went and stood.

Now they are dancing the Deer Dance. At each end of the line they sit, those two who had been their lovers. Now they stand up, they hold their flints.

Toward them the women stretched their hands. They thought, "I should like to touch you!" They touched nothing. They could only see them.

The dance is nearly over. They stand at the ends, the flint-carriers. And one of them walked over. She thought, "I should like to speak to him!" And then she spoke to him, she said, "Why don't you speak to us? We have come so far! We wanted to see you, we wanted you again!"

He said, "I can't speak to you now. Tomorrow I will speak to you."

So, when the dance was over, they went back to where they had first been standing and right there they sat down. At last it grew light. They were still there. They were hungry. No one had come to speak to them as they sat there. Finally, the sun came up. They looked around and found themselves in front of a house, and saw that there was an old woman sitting there. Suddenly, the old woman spoke.

"Are you the ones I've heard them speak of, the living ones with bones?"

"Yes, we are," they said.

Then she said, "Where do you come from?"

"From Katimin."

And she said, "I also came from there. I am the one who was world-maker ten times. Then at Rock Hill Ridge I floated up as a fog."

Then they said, "We too came the same way," and they added, "the Bird brought us."

Then she said to them, "Why did you come here?"

They said, "They were our lovers, the two flint-carriers. That's why we came here. We wanted to talk to them."

Then the old woman said, "I don't think you can do it. It's a great pity for you that you have come so far for nothing. And for only two nights you can stay here. All of them, they don't like you. You have bones."

Then she questioned them about everything. "Katimin, the country, does it look the same?" Then she said, "I'll make a lunch for you when you leave."

They said, "All right."

Then they stayed the day with the old woman. Right there all around they were playing all kinds of gambling games, but the girls never went near. Then, when it was dark, again they made a big fire. They swept the ground well all around.

Then again, the Bird told them, "Go and stand at the ends of the line when the dance is going on. There they, your lovers, will be carrying the flints."

At last, when they were almost ready to stop, as the girls were standing at the ends of the line again, one of the lovers spoke.

He said, "Where are you staying?"

And she said, "Under the eaves of the old woman's house, that's where we're staying."

Then he said, "We will come there when we have finished."

So, when they had finished, the women went back to the house, and soon the men arrived.

Then they said, "It is a great pity that you have come so far for nothing. You can't even touch us. You have bones! There is nothing more that we can say to you."

Then the women told them how they had come there, how they used to go and cry while they looked at the trimmed trees. And then they said, the lovers, "You should not do that anymore. We can never go back there, we have come to have no bones. But, nevertheless, we feel very sad for you. And you must not stay here long. You have bones. And don't eat any food, even if they give it to you." Then the lovers said good-by to them. "And don't grieve for us. We are flint-carriers here, and that is all."

Then the girls said, "We will go back. And we won't eat any food, even if they give it to us."

In the early morning, the Bird said, "You must get ready. We are going to leave."

Then they told the old woman, "We are going to leave."

The old woman tied up the lunch. She wrapped it well with brush. Then she said, "Don't lose it. When you get back, whenever you see someone dying, rub this on his lips. Only when this is gone need anyone ever die again. Right away, people will get well when you rub this on their lips."

Then they said good-by to the old woman and they started out. The Bird left all his children there. They traveled back the same way they had come. Above them flew the Bird. At last, when they had gone very far, again it seemed as though they were going downhill. Suddenly, they looked over and saw the hill they called Farthest-out-One and they thought, "We are nearly there!" At Rock Ridge Hill they ran down and they came to Katimin.

The people had been looking for them everywhere. They were crying, they thought the girls had been killed. They were all amazed when they saw these two coming home.

The Bird went back to the top of the Sugar Loaf. That is his home.

As for what the women brought back with them, before long one died near their home, and they rubbed on his lips what had been given them. He came to life. And, indeed, from that time on, that's the way it happened. Downstream, far away, everywhere, when anyone died they rubbed it on and he came to life. And also upstream, here and there, they rubbed that on and the people came to life. At last, the land on every little creek was occupied and the people were crowded. It was many years before what the old woman had given them was all gone and finally a person died.

The Bird is there yet, and still he takes his children to the land where the spirits go. Only two of them, they live there, one male and one female. Sometimes people kill one of them. Then, in only two days, another will come to take its place. The feathers are medicine for any kind of sickness that may be around. People carry the feathers of the Bird, so that they won't get sick. That's why from time to time they kill one. . . .

CEREMONY FOR RAIN (NILTSA BIKAH NAHAAGHA)

as told to Sidney M. Callaway and Gary Witherspoon

The worship of ecology is a necessity in the deserts of northern Arizona. And so, the ancient Ceremony for Rain of the Navajos is both religious and good farm management. So is the lesson taught by this so-called "myth," which is now part of the curriculum of the tribal-run elementary school at Rough Rock, Arizona, whose all-Navajo School Board includes a learned medicine man as well as university-trained educators. ("Ceremony for Rain," as told to Sidney M. Callaway, Gary Witherspoon, and others, *Grandfather Stories*, Rough Rock, Az., Navajo Curriculum Center, 1970.)

Navajos tell a story about a time many generations ago when it did not rain on their land for several years. The earth became very dry. Many plants and animals died of thirst. The people were short of food. They had only rabbits, squirrels, prairie dogs, deer, and antelope to eat, and many of those animals were dying. There were no crops for food.

After four years without rain, the people became very worried. Gopher (*Na azisi*), who is the go-between among the Earth People (*Nihookaa dine e*) and the Water People (*Niltsa dine e*), knew the bad condition of the Earth People. He wanted to help, so he started digging upward until he reached ground level. There he spread some damp earth which he had pushed up from below the surface.

Humming Bird (*Dah yiitihi*) was the only one who could travel far because the air was thin and there was little water. One day, he found the damp earth which Gopher had pushed up to the surface.

Humming Bird pecked the damp earth and began to dig. He found a tunnel leading downward. Under the surface, he came upon Frog. Humming Bird told Frog about the bad condition on the earth. Frog said that the Water People planned to take the rain away from the Earth People for twelve years because the Earth People had forgotten to use and respect their sacred things and ceremonies. Frog said the Earth People had become dishonest and were destroying many holy things.

Humming Bird asked Frog to give the rain back to the Earth People. Frog said the Earth People could have the rain back if they would make offerings to the Water People and would send someone to the "Place Where the Rivers Meet" (*To ahidlinii*) to see Water Ox (*Teeh Hooltsodii*). [That is where the Los Piños and San Juan Rivers meet. It is today the site of the Navajo Dam.]

Humming Bird returned to the people, carrying some of the damp earth. He told the Earth People about his visit with Frog. He told the Earth People that they were to gather all their precious stones and make an offering to the Water People. He also told them they should send someone to "Where the Rivers Meet" because that was the home of Water Ox.

The Earth People believed the story of Humming Bird. They gathered four precious stones (*nitl iz*) from the four directions. They got turquoise (*dootl izhii*) from the east, abalone (*diichil i*) from the south, white shell (*yoolgaii*) from the west and jet (*baashzhinii*) from the north. Corn pollen was sprinkled on these precious stones while prayers were said and songs were sung.

While others started the ceremony, Talking God (*Haashch eelti i*) was sent to the home of Water Ox at "Where the Rivers Meet." He was to ask Water Ox to give the rain back to the Earth People.

At the rivers where Water Ox lived, Talking God saw tracks of Coyote coming from the east and going into the water. Other tracks showed Coyote also had come out of the water, had gone to the east, and had shaken the water off himself. Talking God went to the place where Coyote had shaken himself. Talking God found a seed of white corn there. Wind told him to pick the corn up, which he did. Then he returned to where the others were making an offering to the Water People.

The next day, the People again sang the songs and said the prayers of the Rain Ceremony. Talking God again went to the rivers where Water Ox had his home. This time, Talking God saw Coyote's tracks coming from the south and going into the water. Other tracks showed that Coyote had come out of the water and had gone a short distance to the south and again had shaken himself. Talking God went to the place where Coyote had shaken himself and found two seeds of blue corn. Wind told him to pick the seeds up, which he did. Then he returned again to the homes of the Earth People.

On the third day, the people continued the ceremony for rain. Talking God again went to the rivers. This time, Coyote had entered the water from the west. As he had left the river area, he again had shaken himself. Talking God found three seeds of yellow corn where Coyote had shaken himself. Wind told him to pick up the seeds of corn, which he did. Then he returned to the home of the Earth People.

On the fourth day, the Rain Ceremony was continued. Talking God again went to the rivers. Coyote had entered the water from the north and had left to the north. Before leaving he had shaken himself. Talking God went to the place where Coyote had shaken himself, and he found many different kinds of seeds. Among them were pumpkin, bean, melon, muskmelon, gourd, etc. Wind told Talking God to pick up the seeds; so Talking God picked them up and took them home with him as he had done with the other seeds. Wind also told Talking God that he should plant the seeds, even though the earth was dry.

Before planting the seeds a one-night Blessingway (*Hozhooji*) Ceremony was performed for the seeds and the precious stones. The people spent the next four days planting the seeds. On the fifth day of planting, Wind told them to send some people to "Where the Rivers Meet" and to

"White River Falls" to make offerings of precious stones to the Water People there. Five people were sent to each place.

The five who were sent to "White Water Falls" were told by the Water People there that they had no control over the rain and that the Water People at "Where the Rivers Meet" had control of the rain. This was partly because Water Ox lived at "Where the Rivers Meet."

The five who went to "Where the Rivers Meet" were more successful. They made an offering of precious stones to the Water People there. A rainbow appeared by the water. Wind told the five people to get on the rainbow. The people did, and it took them down through the water to twelve steps of water. The people went down the twelve steps. There they found Water Ox.

They asked Water Ox to return the rain to above the earth. Water Ox told the Earth People not to worry. He told them to go home and mend their ways of living. He told them to respect their sacred things and ceremonies. He told them not to do things which were wrong and dangerous. He told them to be kind to each other and not to be selfish.

Water Ox also told the five people not to look, for twelve days, at the crops they had planted.

The five people came out of the water on the Stairway of Twelve Steps. They returned to the others and told them about their visit with Water Ox. They said it soon would rain and that the people must start living better. They said no one should look at the crops for twelve days.

The next morning, dark clouds covered the sky. It began to rain. It rained hard for four days. Then it just drizzled for eight more days. The people did not look at their crops.

Finally, the twelfth day arrived. The people went to look

at their crops. They were very happy at what they saw. The seeds had sprouted and were growing rapidly. The rains continued that year, and the people had a large harvest.

Since that time, the Navajos have used the Rain Ceremony when they needed rain badly. This ceremony is usually performed in a person's home with songs and prayers. The offerings of the four precious stones are placed in springs, ponds, rivers, or lakes. The ceremony is performed during the time between the last quarter (*dah iitaago*) and the full moon (*haniibaazgo*).

THE LEGEND OF DR. FEWKES AND MASAUWU

by Edmund Nequatewa

"In the autumn of 1898, the late Dr. Fewkes, archaeologist of the Smithsonian Institution, was staying at Walpi, one of the Hopi Indian Pueblos. In the annual report of the director of the Bureau of Ethnology his visit is noted as follows:

'In November, Dr. J. Walter Fewkes repaired to Arizona for the purpose of continuing his researches concerning the winter ceremonies of the Hopi Indians, but soon after his arrival an epidemic of smallpox manifested itself in such severity as to completely demoralize the Indians and to prevent them from carrying out their ceremonial plans, and at the same time placed Dr. Fewkes in grave personal danger. It accordingly became necessary to abandon the work for the season.'

"The Hopis at Walpi have another story of the cause of Dr. Fewkes' departure."

(From Introduction to "The Legend of Dr. Fewkes," by Edmund Nequatewa in *Truth of the*

Hopi, edited by Mary Russell F. Colton, Museum of
Northern Arizona, 1967, pp. 121–3.)

One of the most important of the Hopi winter ceremonies is
the Wuwuchim, which comes in November. At a certain
time during the ceremony, the One-Horned and the Two-
Horned Societies hold a secret rite in a certain part of the
pueblo, and all the people who live on that plaza go away
and close their houses. No one may witness this ceremony,
for Masauwu, the Earth God, is there with the One-Horned
priests who do his bidding in the Underworld and the spirits
of the dead are there and it is said that anyone who sees
them will be frozen with fright or paralyzed or become like
the dead.

Masauwu owns all the Hopi world, the surface of the
earth, and the Underworld beneath the earth. He is a
mighty and terrible being for he wears upon his head a bald
and bloody mask. He is like death and he clothes himself in
the rawhides of animals and men cannot bear to look upon
his face. The Hopi say he is really a very handsome great
man of a dark color with fine long black hair and that he is
indeed a great giant. When the Hopi came up from the Underworld and looked about them in fear, the first sign which
they saw of any being of human form was the great foot-
prints of Masauwu. Now Masauwu walks only at night and
he carries a flaming torch. Fire is his and he owns the fiery
pits. Every night, Masauwu takes his torch and he starts out
on his rounds, for he walks clear around the edge of the
world every night.

Dr. Fewkes had been in the kiva all day taking notes on
what he saw going on there. Finally, the men told him that
he must go away and stay in his house, for Masauwu was
coming, and that part of the ceremony was very sacred and
no outside person was ever allowed to see what was going

on. They told him to go into his house and lock the door, and not to try to see anything, no matter what happened, or he would be dragged out and he would "freeze" to death. So he went away into his house and he locked the door just as he had been told to do and he sat down and began to write up his notes.

Now, suddenly, he had a queer feeling, for he felt that there was someone in the room, and he looked up and saw a tall man standing before him, but he could not see his face for the light was not good. He felt very much surprised for he knew that he had locked the door.

He said, "What do you want and how did you get in here?" The man replied, "I have come to entertain you."

Dr. Fewkes said, "Go away, I am busy and I do not wish to be entertained."

And, now, as he was looking at the man, he suddenly was not there any more. Then a voice said, "Turn your head a moment," and when the Doctor looked again the figure stood before him once more, but this time its head was strange and dreadful to see.

And the Doctor said, "How did you get in?" and the man answered and said, "I go where I please, locked doors cannot keep me out! See, I will show you how I entered," and, as Dr. Fewkes watched, he shrank away and became like a single straw in a Hopi hair whisk and he vanished through the keyhole.

Now, Dr. Fewkes was very much frightened and, as he was thinking what to do, there was the man back again. So he said once more to him, "What do you want?" and the figure answered as before and said, "I have come to entertain you." So, the Doctor offered him a cigarette and then a match, but the man laughed and said, "Keep your match, I do not need it," and he held the cigarette before his horrible face and blew a stream of fire from his mouth upon it and lit his cigarette. Then, Dr. Fewkes was very much afraid, indeed, for now he knew who it was.

Then the being talked and talked to him, and, finally, the Doctor "gave up to him" and said he would become a Hopi and be like them and believe in Masauwu, and Masauwu cast his spell on him and they both became like little children and all night long they played around together and Masauwu gave the Doctor no rest.

And it was not long after that Dr. Fewkes went away, but it was not on account of the smallpox, as you now know.

Although Dr. Fewkes never reported this story to the outside world, the Hopis now tell that he related it to the priests in the kiva the next day after the strange occurrence. We can see how in less than forty years a legend had its birth.

MANABOZHO AND THE GAMBLER

by Gerald Vizenor

In the cosmos of the tribes there was always the human element of chance, whereby a man or woman influences his or her life by acts of courage or wisdom. Man is finite, not infinite. To the tribal man, "The name of the game is life," says a Lakota educator. The coyote and the trickster tales illustrate this. So do the Manabozho stories of Anishinabe. ("Manabozho and the Gambler," by Gerald Vizenor, *Anishinabe Adisokan*, Minn., Nodin Press, 1970, pp. 147–9.)

Manabozho approached the entrance of this ghastly abode and, raising the mat of scalps which served for a door, found himself in the presence of the *Nita Ataged.* He was a curious-looking being and seemed almost round in shape and

Manabozho thought he could not be a very dexterous gambler who would let himself be beaten by the being who was then grinning at him. Finally, the *Nita Ataged* spoke and said: *So, Manabozho, you, too, have come to try your luck. And you think I am not a very expert gambler.* He grinned and chuckled—a horrible mingling of scorn and ridicule.

Reaching for his war club, he continued: *All those hands you see hanging around this wigwam are the hands of your relatives who came here to gamble. They thought as you are thinking. They played and lost and their life was the forfeit. I seek no one to come and gamble with me but they that would gamble. Seek me and whoever enters my lodge must gamble. Remember, there is but one forfeit I demand of those who gamble with me and lose, and that forfeit is life. I keep the scalps and ears and hands, the rest of the body I give to my friends the windigo and their spirits I consign to Niba Gisiss. I have spoken. Now we will play.*

At the conclusion of this speech, *Manabozho* laughed long and heartily. This was unusual for those who came there to gamble and the *Nita Ataged* felt very uneasy at the stolid indifference of his guest.

Now, said the *Nita Ataged* taking the *pagessewin*—*Anishinabe* dish game—*here are four figures—the four ages of man—which I will shake in the dish four times. If they assume a standing position each time, then I am the winner. Should they fall, then I am the loser.*

Again, *Manabozho* laughed a merry laugh, saying: *Very well, I will play, but it is customary for the party who is challenged to play any game to have the last play.* The *Nita Ataged* consented to do this. Taking up the dish, he struck it a sharp, quick blow on a spot prepared for the purpose on the ground. The figures immediately assumed a standing position. This was repeated three times, and each time the figures stood erect in the dish. But one chance remained, upon which depended the destiny of *Manabozho* and the salvation of the *Anishinabe* people.

He was not frightened, and when the *Nita Ataged* prepared to make the final shake, *Manabozho* drew near and when the dish came down on the ground he made a whistle on the wind, as in surprise, and the figures fell. *Manabozho* then seized the dish, saying: *It is now my turn. Should I win, you must die.*

▲▲▲▲▲▲▲▲▲▲▲▲▲▲▲▲▲▲▲

III. THE NEW INDIANS

THE RESERVATIONS

Of the not quite two billion acres that Indians once inhabited, the U.S. government permits tribes to reside on only 56 million acres. This land is "critically eroded" (14 million acres), or "severely eroded" (17 million acres), or "slightly eroded" (25 million acres). Nonetheless, this is the most religiously sacred and blasphemed against land in the country, as made clear by a young Apache girl ("What Is an Indian Reservation?" by Marilyn Cosen, *Akwesasne Notes*, Vol. I, No. 7, July, 1969), and an old Cupeno woman ("We Do Not Want Any Other Home," by Celsa Apapas, *Aboriginal American Oratory*, p. 115.)

What Is an Indian Reservation?

by Marilyn Cosen, White Mountain Apache

A reservation is a source of security to the Indian. I say this because there he can feel free—freedom in practicing his own customs. Another thing is his land. I think one's environment has a great effect on the person—to the Indian, his land is his own. His ancestors inhabited that land; he was brought up on that land; he knows it; he claims it. What if the reservations were abolished? Then the land would be open for different causes and the Indian would be "lost." I'm not saying that reservations should not be abolished, so that the Indian can practice his part in the reservation communities and learn how to deal with Indian problems and, most important of all, preserve his culture.

We Do Not Want Any Other Home

by Celsa Apapas

You asked us to think what place we like next best to this place, where we always lived. You see that graveyard out there? There are our fathers and our grandfathers. You see that Eagle-nest Mountain and that Rabbit-hole Mountain? When God made them, He gave us this place. We have always been here. We do not care for any other place. . . . If you give us the best place in the world, it is not so good for us as this. . . . This is our home. . . . We cannot live anywhere else. We were born here and our fathers are buried here. . . . We want this place and not any other. . . .

There is no other place for us. We do not want you to buy any other place. If you will not buy this place, we will go into the mountains like quail, and die there, the old people and the women and children. Let the Government be glad and proud. It can kill us. We do not fight. We do what it says. If we cannot live here, we want to go into the mountains and die. We do not want any other home.

ON AN INDIAN RESERVATION: HOW COLONIALISM WORKS

by Robert K. Thomas

In 1872, the Commissioner of Indian Affairs, Francis Walker, declared, "There is no question of national dignity, be it remembered, involved in the treatment

of savages by a civilized power." The purpose of the
reservation system, said the Commissioner, was to re-
duce "the wild beasts [the Indians] to the condition of
supplicants for charity." How the reservation system
has evolved in modern times is discussed by an anthro-
pologist of the Cherokee tribe. ("Colonialism: Classic
and Internal," by Robert Thomas, *New University
Thought*, Vol. IV, No. 4, Winter, 1966–7, pp. 39–43.)

An Indian reservation is the most complete colonial system
in the world that I know about. One of the things you find
on Indian reservations is exploitation of natural resources.
(Now, I don't want to give you the impression that the U.S.
government goes out with big imperialist designs on Indian
reservations. Were it that simple, were there nice, clean-cut
villains, you could just shoot them or something. But it isn't
that simple.) Let us say that the U.S. government is in
charge of the resources on an Indian reservation and cuts
the timber. You have a "tribal sawmill," which is tribal only
in the sense that it is located on the reservation, but people
in the government bureaucracy actually run it. They're supposed to. They are legally told to do that and they have no
choice. They aren't being "mean" to the Indians, they're
just supposed to run the sawmill. If they don't run it, they
lose their jobs, that's all.

So, the people who tend to get the jobs in the sawmill are
the "responsible" Indians. Now, you can imagine who the
responsible Indians are. They are people who are most like
the whites in many ways, and hence the most "cooperative," that is, they keep their mouths shut and their noses
clean. This makes for bitter factionalism on many reservations, and is another outcome of this classic colonial structure. Accordingly, this kind of structure always creates an
economic elite of *marginal people*, or cooperative marginal

people. I don't want to give you the impression that all marginal people on all Indian reservations or in all countries around the world are economic elites, they aren't. (Sometimes, if they are marginal enough, they become revolutionaries.) But this is one class of people created by the classic colonial structure.

When the resources are sold and the returns go into the tribal treasury, the people who have control of it, insofar as anybody on the Indian reservation has control of anything, are these marginal people. Their job is to mediate between the Indian Bureau and the Indians, and they are the same people who work in the sawmill. They have very little power beyond that which the Bureau will give them. The raw materials from this reservation are, of course, sold outside of the reservation area. The U.S. government deducts from the sales of these resources the costs of providing social services to the reservation. (If any of you are familiar with the head-tax system in Africa and Asia, for instance, you can see a very close resemblance.) The remaining money goes into the tribal treasury and, in turn, is allocated to further economic activity which is first planned and then sanctioned by the government as before. What happens after a little while, what is bound to happen, is that the natural resources of this region are drained off. So, in a sense, you don't have economic change there at all.

What does an Indian experience in this situation? You have to make decisions in order to have experience, and few if any decisions here are taken by Indians.

Let's take another example: an industry that moves into an Indian reservation. I was on the Pine Ridge Indian reservation when a fishhook plant was brought in. The Bureau administrators thought that this was good for the reservation because it would create jobs and bring in money. Buildings were built to lure in industry. After the buildings were finished and the industry moved in, people were found to help recruit the labor for the industry. Because of the high transportation costs, the wages were not high, but, in the minds of the administrators, it was better than nothing—although many people referred to them as sweat shops.

So, they are now making fishhooks on the Pine Ridge reservation. Sioux males were recruited to provide the labor for the industry—to tie fishhooks. Do any of you know anything about the Sioux Indians? Well, they were the finest light cavalry the world has ever seen, the finest military organization, and the finest warriors in the world. They are also the most thin-skinned men you've ever met—they'll hit you in the mouth at the drop of a hat. And they're supposed to tie feathers onto fishhooks? Not likely. So, right away it was defined as women's work—nice little ladies putting nice little feathers on nice little fishhooks. So, the Sioux men quit. This means they are faced with alternatives of being defined as irresponsible slobs by the people who are promoting industry, or as sissies by their own fellows—that's a big choice! You can either go in and tie those feathers to those fishhooks, while your buddies are out punching cattle—a man's job—or you can be an irresponsible slob, not providing for your families again.

And that is what happens in most colonial countries right across the world—the communty lies inert until prodded. That's what happens after a long history of not having experience, you lie inert until prodded, i.e., nobody at the bottom or even among the intermediaries acts until someone at the top acts in a way that you must respond.

And you are judged on how you respond. So, if a man from the top or intermediary group comes and asks you whether or not you're going to work in a fishhook factory and you answer yes, then the rest of the community judges you on that reaction. They consider you a "white man's Indian," say. And after a certain amount of time people can only respond in terms of this structure and its movements, because all the institutions, information, and experience is located there.

Let's look at the cattle program. Every once in a while the U.S. decides it should sponsor an economic-agricultural activity. The government gives money to the people whose job it is to mediate between the government and the people. If you're on an Indian tribal council, you look to those people to tell you how to set up a program. How else could you do that? You've never seen a cattle program. You've never run one. You've never taken action very much yourself except in terms of waiting for these people to give you cues so you can act negatively or positively. Now you find out how to set up a cattle program. You set up a cattle program and you make individual loans. The intermediaries run the loan board, again because they are more like white men by virtue of their association with them—not because of their experience in making decisions for this community, but just because of their association with whites outside of the formal institutional context. So they run the loan board and then Sam Blackbird, say, comes in and wants to get a loan—a big strappin' Sioux Indian about thirty-two who's worked about two years since he was fifteen and the rest of the time he's lived with his folks. Well, you're not going to give money to Sam Blackbird. Suppose, for some unknown reason, Sam Blackbird would get a loan. Everybody would come over and say, "Gee, Sam, how lucky can you get—them guys up there finally gave you some money, so let's cut out one of these big steer here and eat it." Well, what is Sam going to do? He can act like a "lousy, greedy white man," which is what Indians think white men are—not be a Sioux, in other words—or he can default on his loan. Those are the options that the structure offers him.

Now, in fact, what would happen is that Sam Blackbird would kill the steer and default on his loan. So, if you're going to start a cattle program in this community that isn't the way you would do it. But nobody in the community really knows that, because nobody has ever run a cattle program, and it's been so long since anybody ever did anything like a cattle program that there are really no analogies to call on—they would just have to experiment around to find out how to run a cattle program, which they are not able to do. (As a social scientist, I could just make a guess, it would be only a guess, that a group of brothers should be given financial responsibility and that might work. But, I don't know, it's been too long since this institution has functioned and decisions have been in their hands. Africa was never in this bad shape—the reservation is the most complete system of colonialism I know.)

Let me go back to the first point that I made about these two processes of change. What I've been talking about is really lack of change because the structure isolates the people from experience. Let me give you an example of how that could be different.

There was a small industry started by the University of Chicago among the Sac and Fox in Tama, Iowa. And it was a mess—everybody got mad right away. I remember I went out there one time and everybody had just walked off their jobs because somebody had said something to somebody (this is a kinship society, a tribe in which interpersonal relations are the most important thing). But they came back the next day because they also wanted the industry. In any case, all kinds of things changed at Tama—and really changed.

Before the project, an Indian might work in Marshalltown, Iowa, say—and maybe an uncle would come over one day and say, "Joe, I want to go into town and buy some birthday gifts for my little niece, would you take me into town?" Joe has twenty minutes to go to work, but do you know what he does? He takes his uncle into town. He shows up the next day and the foreman says, "Where were you on Monday?" And he says, "I had to take my uncle into town." And the foreman says, "Holy mackerel, I've got a production deadline, and you have to take your uncle to town!" So he says, "Pick up your check, pal, you're through." And Joe's reaction is, "Well, those white people are mean, everybody knows that." So, he goes home. And then he has to wait another year before he ventures out to get another job.

Well, one of the things the Sac and Fox found out working in the project industry was that, if you went over and asked your nephew to take you into town at the time he was supposed to go up and work with the rest of his kinfolk, then all the other kinfolk got mad at you for asking him to do that. And that's the way that they learned about production deadlines. And they learned it. (Tribal people can be coercive. They are not only friendly, smiling folk people. That's one side of them. They can also be mean as hell, and can put social controls on you like nobody's business.)

Here is another example. One of the Indians was in the process of drawing a sketch for a tile (the kind you put under hot things) when his uncle died. He was supposed to go into a four-day seclusion. It was two months before Christmas, with the Christmas rush coming up. Everybody wondered what they could do: "Charlie has to go into four-day seclusion. We're going to miss all this stuff for Christmas." So they went to their own priest. They sat around. Then he said, "Why don't you fix a little place under the door so Charlie can make those designs and slip 'em out under the door. He doesn't have to touch anybody, or see anybody." And they worked that out so that Charlie could keep on working.

Now, that's experience and change. That's facing other

kinds of people and your environment in terms of your own aspirations and in terms of the kind of life you're leading.

Let me give you another example. In the early days of the project, they needed to organize industry, but these are tribal people, all relatives, and nobody likes to tell anybody else what to do. So, they got together and decided they're going to nominate someone for chairman because they've heard that whites do that sort of thing. So they nominate Dan, say, who almost crawls under the desk at the thought of having to tell his relatives what to do. So, then, everybody realizes maybe that isn't going to work so well, and they decide to abandon it. Finally, they figure out that the guy who had the most hours in the previous year would become chairman of the board in the industry. By the nature of the case, he didn't have to volunteer, the one with the most hours just had the job. Now, I would never have thought of that. Never in a million years. But that is what I mean about experience and change. Under the colonial system, it doesn't happen. It can't. Of course, the situation on an American Indian reservation is extreme, because a large part of the environment that the American Indian faces are American whites.

Let me now return to the two elements of change, decay of institution and social isolation. When you have peasant people and institutions decay, it looks to me that you just get bigger and better intermediaries, marginal men. When an urban person's institutions decay, and by urban I mean middle-class, he is blocked off from coming true. It gives him identity problems. Institutions for him are not so much where he makes decisions about jobs and environment, although that's true, too, but he makes decisions about himself in those institutions. But tribal people—and this is true of a lot of Africans, Asians, and American Indians—who have their structure taken away are in bad shape because they respond to structure. You know, in the beginning, God said, "We are the people who plant corn," or something of that sort. What you are is defined, given. It is defined in ritual. It is defined in interaction. You take away the institutions and tribal people (and I mean this literally, and, believe me, I know, because I come from a conservative tribal background and I went through this) will do whatever is most pleasurable under the circumstances. If they like to drink, they'll drink themselves right into oblivion. There are whole American Indian tribes who are just drinking themselves into oblivion. And I don't think that there is any particular psychological trouble unless whites look at that and tell them it's bad. Then there's trouble.

OUR BENEFACTOR, THE BIA: INDIAN VERSION OF THE LORD'S PRAYER

Anonymous

> "The Great White Ultimate Trustee—myself," former Secretary of Interior Stewart Udall, jokingly referred to his Cabinet responsibility for overseeing the Bureau of Indian Affairs (BIA). In mocking reply, a young Indian wrote the anonymous "Indian Version of the Lord's Prayer" to the "Great White Father" in the Bureau of Indian Affairs. (*The Native Nevadan*, Vol. V, No. 8, Dec. 2, 1968, p. 1.)

Our benefactor in Indian Affairs
Hallowed by thy position
Thy downfall comes,
With every election
Thy will be done on this reserve
As will be done on every other reserve.

Give us this day our daily rations
And forgive us our trespasses as we will
Forgive you your trespasses on our land.
Lead us not into integration
But deliver us from exploitation.
For thine is the establishment, the power, and the glory.
For as long as the grass shall grow
And the rivers flow and the sun shines.
Forever and ever—unh!

THE DOG PROBLEM

by the editor, Maine Indian Newsletter

Legally, the Indians are "wards of the government."
That is, tribal land and money are "held in trust" by
the BIA. "It is very difficult to get away from complete
paternalism under this relationship," said Commissioner of Indian Affairs, Robert Bennett. In the *Har-
vard Law Record*, Ralph Nader commented, in 1964:
"Telling the Indians when to go to bed and when to
get up is not just a whimsical bit of paternalism. It has
deep roots in a long tradition of Indian Bureau policy"—
as this article about dog licenses on the Passamaquoddy Reservation, in Maine, indicates. ("Comments
and Observations," by the editor, *Maine Indian Newsletter*, Vol. III, No. 6, Feb., 1969, p. 3.)

Recently, a legislative hearing was held at which Commissioner Hinckley was questioned regarding a dog ordinance
which the Passamaquoddy want put into law. (This law is
similar to the one the Penobscots already have.) The hearing
was long for something so simple. Overheard was a report-
er's comment, "If it takes them this long to discuss a dog or-

dinance, what do they do when they have something really important?" Hinckley was asked if it wasn't too cruel to shoot a dog which was not properly licensed; it was suggested that the dogs might be taken to a dog pound. To this, Hinckley replied that Ellsworth was the nearest place to take them and it was over 100 miles away from the reservation. Hinckley was then asked, "You mean you don't have any means to care for these dogs on the reservation?" Hinckley explained then that we don't even have the means to take care of *people* on the reservation, let alone dogs.

There is no human solution to this dog problem. Shooting a child's unlicensed dog seems cruel and it would seem proper that at least one warning be given the owner and a reasonable time to have the dog licensed before carrying out this maximum penalty.

It must be remembered that only the people living on the reservation know if the number of dogs running around is sufficient to constitute a general nuisance, and their wishes on this matter should be respected. Before this bill was submitted to the legislature, just like all of the other Indian bills submitted to the legislature, it was discussed by the tribal governors and councils and agreed upon. These governors and council members are elected officials of their respective tribal reservations. Council meetings are usually open meetings and any member of the tribe who wishes may come and ask questions and make statements, so, when all is said and done, it is the Indian people themselves who know that a problem exists and know how best to deal with it. tahu.

ALWAYS AGAINSTING MY HUSBAND
ALBERT HAINOIS AND EVERYTHING,
OR UNEMPLOYED FOREVER

by Anna Hainois

> On the reservations unemployment *averaged* from 45
> to 95 percent during the decade of the 1960's. The sta-
> tistics vary, the unemployment does not. "Public
> Enemy No. 1 [is] Poverty," said the Navajo leader,
> Howard McKinley. The degrading effect of unemploy-
> ment in daily life is here described by a Maine Indian
> woman. (*Maine Indian Newsletter*, Vol. III, No. 3,
> Nov., 1968, pp. 9–10.)

Always againsting my husband Albert Hainois and everything. Trying to earn money for the family. The Director of
CAP and the Governor are the ones who giving us hard time.
When he bought the tractor, he couldn't get a job from
Georgia Pacific because the Governor was against him. I
called Augusta State House to the Indian Commission and I
called the Indian Agent. And they were the ones that got
my husband's job Georgia Pacific. And in my point of view
nobody else deserves the credit except them. They were the
only two men I got help from. I even asked the CAP director
for help and he didn't even know how to call Augusta. Until
after he heard that I called the Indian Commissioner. He
called up, but I already called first. And again my husband
asked for a job as a skidder operator. So this CAP director
came along with my husband's record. Saying over to my
sister's place Albert couldn't get a job because of a bad record. And that's the reason why my husband couldn't get a
job. And the CAP director also said my husband quit for no
reason at all.

The reason why he quit so many times is because I've had

eight children and two children I had to be operated on. And he has to stay at home to take care of the children. Cause we couldn't find a baby sitter. And I had three other operations. And he had to stay home. Some men quit for no reason at all. Still right today they are working for the same company they quit from. The CAP director had only my husband's record. What about the other records? As far as I'm concern, nobody has a good record not even the CAP from up here in Dana Point. Some men don't stay home and take care of children still they quit. So you see nobody has a good record. This CAP director thinks he's Mr. Know It All. But he doesn't know my husband's reasons.

But they always find an excuse for my husband in order not to earn money. Before I was operated on five months ago, my husband was cutting cedar. The Governor and the CAP director took the cedar without my husband's consent. My husband wouldn't have known the cedar was stolen till one of the men told me and afterwards we knew the whole story about the cedar. They had to transport the cedar back. So you see how they go against my husband no matter what he does. Right now he's working for my sister to pay for his bills. I hope nobody goes over there and tells my sister Albert has a bad record so don't give him a job. The CAP doesn't even have a good record about everything. And I mean just the CAP up here in Dana Point. They giving repairs to a man who lives alone and is selling the stuff cheap: doors $4, windows $2, storm windows $2. And that's very, very cheap. Last week a woman told us she didn't get any repairing she asked for. She has three children and she's taking care of her brothers and sister. She's the one who needs the repairing, not this man who's selling the stuff so cheap. Maybe this man is a CAP special. This sounds like a special menu. So now I have to close my long truthful letter. So men don't ever quit on a job. Think about your record or else you'll be unemployed forever like my husband Albert Hainois.

INDIAN HUMOR

> Vine Deloria, Jr., in his *Custer Died for Your Sins* (New York, Macmillan), wrote, "Indians have found a humorous side to every problem." But, the combination of verbal slapstick and social comment has a double cutting edge, as seen in "A Cherokee Joke," *The New Indians,* by Stan Steiner, New York, Harper & Row, 1968; "Etiquette of the Marriage Bed," *The Plains of the Great West,* by Col. Richard Irving Dodge, p. 305; "Dog Head Stew," by Dorothy Pennington, *Indian Center News,* Vol. VII, No. 1, Sept., 1969; and "The Indian Glossary," *ABC—Americans Before Columbus,* National Indian Youth Council, undated.

A Cherokee Joke: "Watch That Shit!"

An old Cherokee was given an allotment of land, good land, up near Claremont, by mistake. He settled on it and was just about getting ready to be happy when he found out he had a tenant farmer on his land, who was white. Well, they got along fine, for a few weeks. Until the haying began. The tenant farmer did the haying, since he was the tenant farmer, and the old Cherokee just sat around and told him what to do, since he was the landowner.

Now the tenant farmer thought that was peculiar, because it was. Everyone knew Indians sat around because they were lazy, not because they were bosses.

Well, they got the hay into the barn, where it belonged. You know how hay gives off a gas when it's new-cut. Well, they got to sitting around in the barn after the haying, and the white tenant farmer was smoking. So the old Cherokee said to him, "Better not smoke in the barn." The white tenant farmer he grunted, and he nodded. But after the old Cherokee had left the barn he stood up and he said, "Hell, I ain't gonna let no Indian tell me what to do!" And he lit another cigarette. Well, poof! The hay lit and the barn exploded. "Serves him right, all right," the white tenant farmer snorted.

The old Cherokee's dogs heard the explosion and they came running and the white tenant farmer, he shot them. And the old Cherokee's wife came running, and he shot her too. He was getting real mad by then. So he cut the old Cherokee's cows' throats, he set fire to his house, he cut the old truck tires, and he lit out, to make his way in the world.

When the old Cherokee come home and seen his hay gone, his barn burned, his dogs shot, his wife shot, his house set on fire, his cows dead, and his old truck's tires cut, he was pretty annoyed.

"I will get that man for this, if it's the last thing I do on the earth," the old Cherokee said.

So for the next five years the old Cherokee roamed the earth in search of the white tenant farmer. One day he saw a man who looked just like him sitting under a glacier, up near Fairbanks, Alaska, just outside of town by the Dairy Queen stand, where the road forked. He walked up to him and he sat down beside him and he said, "Ain't you the bastard who lit my hay, burned my barn, shot my dogs, shot my wife, set fire to my house, slit the throats of my cows, and cut my old truck's tires?"

"Yep, that's me," the white tenant farmer snorted.

The old Cherokee he looked him right in the eye for a long while, and then he said, "You better watch that shit!"

Etiquette of the Marriage Bed

Spotted Tail came on a visit to the post, and the doctor was specially attentive and hospitable to the Indian chief. One night, the doctor and Spotted Tail came into a room in which were assembled several officers. The doctor was jocose, full of fun, rallying the Indian on his manners and customs, on his having several wives, etc. Spotted Tail stood it for some time. At last, he said, "Doctor, you come to my camp, I give you plenty to eat, good bed, and wife to sleep with. I have been in your camp three days, and you no say wife to me once." It is impossible to describe the horror depicted in the doctor's face. He soon made an excuse to leave, and his close intimacy with Spotted Tail was at least suspended.

Dog Head Stew (For Fifty People)
by Dorothy Pennington

Carefully prepare one medium dog head, removing teeth from jaw bones and hair, putting these aside for future use. Into kettle, add heaping handfuls of camos bulbs and cattail roots. The eggs from two medium-size salmon may be combined with water to cover, and place over fire and bring to boil for three hours.

It is customary to observe the rites of preparation in order to have all present appreciate the dish that will begin the feast.

At the proper moment, using the ceremonial arrow, impale the dog head and bring forth for all to observe the excellence of the dish.

Then allow fifteen to thirty minutes for all whites to excuse themselves and leave for home. Bury stew in back yard and bring forth the roasted turkey with all the trimmings. In this way, a 15-pound turkey will do. The others have been invited to the feast . . . and the fact they didn't stay is their tough luck.

The Indian Glossary

Indian Reservation—our land set aside for us "as long as the grass shall grow and the rivers flow" to be used by non-Indian cattlemen for low-cost grazing, for highways, for dam sites by the Army Engineers.

Uncle Tomahawks—Indian leaders satisfied with the *status quo.*

BIA Official—an important guy wearing a beaded bolo tie.

OEO—a state of confusion.

Indian Problem—the white man's burden.

Integration—marrying into another tribe.

Assimilation—marrying a non-Indian.

10-year Program—a BIA staff program for bettering reservation conditions approved by tribal officials.

"Culturally Deprived"—the suburban white child.

Social Worker—an overtrained, underexposed professional who helps us solve all our problems.

Agency Town—three separate communities in one—BIA, US-PHS, Indian—living side by side with no intercommunication.

Pilot Project—an old project with a new name.

Indian Politician—a guy who, when confronted with a problem he finds he cannot straighten out, messes the situation up good!

Middle-class Indian—a person happily lost in the
"mainstream of American life" who does not claim to be
an Indian until his tribe wins a claims case, then enrolls
all his children in the tribe and fights for a per capita
payment.

THE SPEECH I DIDN'T GIVE WHEN I DIDN'T ADDRESS THE NATIONAL PRESS CLUB, LAST TIME I WAS IN WASHINGTON

by Hank Adams

> In the winter of 1971, Hank Adams was shot in the
> stomach while helping Indian fishermen tend their
> nets on the Nisqually River. Adams, a young Assini-
> boin-Sioux, had for years led the fish-ins, defending
> fishing rights granted by the Treaty of Medicine Creek
> in 1853, but denied the tribes by the courts. Hundreds
> of Indians had been arrested, fishing camps raided and
> destroyed, boats impounded, and Indian fishermen
> shot at, since the fish-ins began in 1964. But Adams
> did not lose his savagely sophisticated sense of humor.
> ("The Speech I Didn't Give," by Hank Adams, unpub-
> lished and undated.)

(*Author's note:* several complaints have been received
about reprinting speeches given at various conferences. In
response, we here include a speech that wasn't given. We
hope we satisfy all complaints.)

It's hard to believe that the six of you have managed to
build such a reputation of prestige for the Press Club. Big

audiences don't frighten me, however—in fact, this reminds me of the last time I appeared before the full membership of a national Indian organization.

But I can understand why you tunnel out in force today, 'cause in the past year Indians have been big news. . . .

In some ways, you may not believe it, congressmen and newsmen are alike. A few years ago, at hearings and at news conferences, everybody used to ask if there weren't any "young, articulate, English-speaking Indians." Now they ask us if there aren't any "old, long-hair, blanket-bearing, Indian-speaking Indians." They say that's all we "need to be effective."

Photographers always say, "Too bad you weren't in costume. You would have went national."

Whenever they say that, we are in costume.

We could have went national with a demonstration of red power last December. We planned to cut down the "National Christmas Tree," leaving behind a tomahawk—and a note saying we didn't do it.

It wasn't the fear of white wrath that stopped us, however, but a threat from NCAI—that is, the "Not Caucasians, but Anglicized Indians."

They told us, "Red Power is Responsible Power."

We told them, if they were talking about what they'd been exercising, then, "Red Power is No Power."

They protested our youthful cynicism, asking, "Do you know how many men adopted by our tribes in the past fifty years have later been elected President of the United States?"

"Ten!" they answered. "Now, that's Red Power!!!"

So you can understand why everybody got mad at us when we picketed the White House in February. We were reduced to picketing when they wouldn't let us send him a message direct. Probably just as well. With our accuracy and his luck—which are about the same—the arrow probably would have hit him. And what the hell would Hubert care if we threatened to take back Lady Bird's Indian name if they didn't come up with something better than the "omnibus" bust. [President Johnson sought to reform Indian affairs through an Omnibus Bill, which the tribes nicknamed the Ominous Bill—eds.]

We should be working at a lower level, anyhow. And if Bob Bennett [Commissioner of Indian Affairs] could ever overcome the handicap of being Bob Bennett, he'd be a swell guy to work with. But we can't disregard him either, because some day he might be in a position of influence. . . .

We could just forget about politics and a lot of other things if there were just 22 million of us. Then a good number of us could make six-digit livings just by telling jokes about the National Congress of American Indians. Not jokes really—the truth would do it. As it is, only about 900 people have ever heard of them—and less than 1% of those are Indian.

THE MAINSTREAM: INDIANS AS HUMAN BEINGS

by Earl Old Person

"Termination" of the reservations and an end to federal treaty obligations to the tribes have been advocated by some as a means to encourage the Indian people to enter "the mainstream of American life." Earl Old Person, a tribal chairman of the Blackfoot Indians of Montana and president of the National Congress of American Indians, writes that the equivalent to "termination" in the Indian languages is "to 'wipe out' or 'kill off,' " and "mainstream" translates as "a big, wide river." Would you "throw [us] into the Big, Wide River?" he asks. (*Integrated Education*, Issue 26, Vol. V, No. 2, April–May, 1967, pp. 18–21.)

It cannot be denied that every time the Bureau of Indian Affairs goes to Congress for money, they justify their request for appropriations on the grounds that they are trying to "get themselves out of the Indian Business." This means termination to members of Congress and to Indians.

It is important to note that in our Indian language the only translation for termination is "to 'wipe out' or 'kill off.' " We have no Indian words for termination. . . .

You have caused us to jump every time we hear this word. We made treaties with the U.S. Government which guaranteed our rights to develop our reservations and to develop as a people free from interference. In order to bring about this development, careful planning must be done on the part of not only the agencies of government, but by the tribes themselves.

But how can we plan our future when the Indian Bureau constantly threatens to wipe us out as a race? It is like trying to cook a meal in your tipi when someone is standing outside trying to burn the tipi down.

So, let's agree to forget the termination talk and instead talk of development of Indian people, their land, and their culture.

Why is it so important that Indians be brought into the "mainstream of American life?" What is the "mainstream of American life"? I would not know how to interpret the phrase to my people in our language. The closest I would be able to come to "mainstream" would be to say, in Indian, "a big, wide river." Am I then to tell my people that they will be "thrown into the Big, Wide River of the United States?"

As first Americans, we had a truly American way of life. And we mixed this with the way of the white man who came to live among us. The result is the most democratic form of government in the world. . . .

We send our best educated delegates to these meetings [of the government—eds.] so they can understand what is being said. We are forced to leave at home the poor and the least educated. We try to put on a good face at these meetings, but we cannot cover up the fact that the pride of our people make them elect those of us who they think have the education and ability to deal with Government officials and the outside world.

Our people are eager to learn. They are proud of being Americans. They are proud of being Indians. They are proud to welcome non-Indians onto the reservation. We feel that we have dealt with honor with the Government through the many treaties we have made. We respect these treaties and expect the Government to do the same. We do not demonstrate in the streets to get our rights. We feel we have rights guaranteed to us by these treaties and we trust the Government to respect these rights.

And what will it cost for the Indian Bureau and the Congress to say, "Go home and develop your plans. You do not have to be afraid to take the time you need. We are not going to sell your land out from under you or force your people off the reservation"?

If this is done, the time will surely come when Indian people everywhere can say in both word and deed that a special agency to handle their affairs is no longer needed.

RELOCATION

by Reverend Watt Spade and Willard Walker

As many as fifty percent of the estimated one million and a half Indians in America are thought to live in urban areas. Relocation—the multimillion-dollar government program of job-training and urban adjustment—yearly entices thousands of reservation Indians to undertake the trek to the cities. One such journey is told in this sardonic tale. (*Cherokee Stories*, by Reverend Watt Spade and Willard Walker, pp. 16–17.)

One time I went up there to Chicago where my brother lives. Rabbit is his name. He was right there when I got off the bus. We were a little hungry, so we stopped to eat on the way across town. This restaurant we stopped at was all glass on the outside, like one big window. You could see all the people eating inside. They weren't sitting down, either; they were all standing up at a counter that wound all around through the place. They were standing along both sides of this counter, but they didn't seem to be talking to each other or looking at each other. It was like they were all looking at the wall.

My brother and I decided to eat at a place called Wally's Bar over near where he lives at Fullerton and Green. There were a lot of people in that place and they were all very friendly. They all seemed to know my brother, too, but they called him "Indian Joe." I hadn't ever heard him called that.

Rabbit told me he didn't have any place where I could stay. He had an apartment, but they'd had a fire there a few days before. We went over to look at it, and I guess he hadn't been there for a few days, because there was a letter from Momma on the stairs right where you come in. There was black soot on the stairs all the way up to the fourth floor, where his apartment was; and there were some Puerto Rican guys up there cleaning the place up. They had the radio turned on real loud playing some kind of Puerto Rican music. The whole place smelled like charcoal and burnt furniture.

We went back to that place where they all called Rabbit "Indian Joe" and I told him about the news from home. Then he told me all about the city and about Chicago Rawhide, where he works. Finally, I said I didn't think I was ready to settle down there just yet. We went on back to the bus station and waited around for the bus back to Oklahoma. There were a couple of Indian guys there, and they were telling this story. They said the government wanted to put a man on the moon and it could be done all right, but nobody knew how to get the guy home again after he landed on the moon. These guys said all the government had to do was put an Indian in that rocket ship and tell him he was being relocated and then, after he got to the moon, that Indian would find his own way home again and the government wouldn't have to figure that part out at all.

Rabbit and I sure liked that story. I wonder what ever happened to those two Indian guys.

ON THE ROAD, INDIAN-STYLE:
THE NEW MIGRATIONS

Three Poems *by Simon Ortiz*

In the old days, bands of Indians migrated, from winter to summer, wherever the pastures and game were plentiful. The young tribesmen follow the ancient trails, on the highways, by car and by bus. Simon Ortiz, of the Acoma Pueblo in New Mexico, and editor of the Navajo *Rough Rock News*, has chronicled this superhighway odyssey in his poems "Relocation," "Missing that Indian Name of Roy or Ray," and "West: Grants to Gallup, New Mexico."

Relocation

don't talk to me no words
don't frighten me
for i am in the blinding city
the lights
the cars
the deadened glares
    tear my heart
    & close my mind

who questions my pain
the tight knot of anger
in my breast
i swallow hard and often
and taste my spit
and it does not taste good
who questions my mind

i came here because i was tired
the BIA taught me to cleanse myself
daily to keep a careful account of my time
efficiency was learned in catechism
the sisters spelled me god in white
and i came here to feed myself
corn & potatoes and chili and mutton
did not nourish me it was said

so i agreed to move
i see me walking in sleep
down streets down streets grey with cement
and glaring glass and oily wind
armed with a pint of wine
i cheated my children to buy
i am ashamed
i am tired
i am hungry
i speak words
i am lonely for hills
i am lonely for myself

Missing That Indian Name of Roy or Ray

1.
can't even remember his name
maybe it was Roy, or Ray,
tell Leslie that,
drinking on Des Moines to K. C. bus,
throbbing with dull nerves,
going home, coming home,
talk to nobody until K. C. depot.
    Meet Roy,
he's wobbling down from Chicago bus
first I see him.
Ya-ta-heh, where you from?
Sanders.
I know where Sanders is.
West of Gallup right off 66.

Two Indians going for a drink.
Wink at a barmaid. Two whiskies

two beers settle down warm
but in a hurry. Look for danger.
In the early morning, when it's getting light,
we're outside of Tulsa, and you see those oil wells,
pumping the juice, the nodding bastards.
Up and down, up and down, all day, getting rich.
On the outskirts, we see a sign:
        Tulsa Screw Products, Co., and laugh and laugh.

2.
He gets lost in Amarillo.
Went to get a couple of hamburgers
and then didn't show back up.
"Where's that Indian that was back there?"
the bus driver asked.
"Went to get some hamburgers," I told him.
And then ran around the block,
but couldn't find him.
At least he took his expensive transistor
with him.
Me and the black guy and the hippie girl
keep looking out the back window
when we pull out of Amarillo.

3.
The black guy gets off in Tucumcari.
Roy, Navajo, coming from places,
new levis, new shirt, everything new,
right in style man, don't talk English
too good, but fuck it, and expensive transistor
we listen to. That's okay, brother,
I like cowboy music, sentimental bullshit,

go to dances at Milan's in Gallup,
saw somebody getting laid out in back once,
saw somebody get knifed there too,
red blood black and shiny in neon light,
quick footsteps running away,
me and my buddy careful to approach him,
don't touch him, and then make a phone call.

Later on in the bus he sings me Navajo songs.
Squaw dance singing, you sing when there's
a crowd, girls, some wine, and fires
that smell good. "Give me two dollars.
                    "And I will like you."
A black guy and a hippie-looking girl
come and join us in the back.
                    "No more dollar.
                    "No more dollar."
And I wonder that it's a strange place
for a black man to get off at.
Tucumcari.

4.
When I get off in Albuquerque
the girl stays on. "See you
           in Portland," she says.
And I walk up the street
missing that Indian we left
behind in Amarillo.

West: Grants to Gallup, New Mexico

Grants, okie town and texans
from the oil fields, come to dig uranium,
grease trucks and run the pumps,
Milan, some long time traveling from Italy.
    West,
        trucks busting ass, gears hot,
        sawmill this side of Prewitt,
west for California,
Thoreau, gas station and bar,
Navajos outside, pass on by
        west, going on
        see you on the way back,
then Top of The World, Real Indian Village,
reptiles, moccasins, postcards, restrooms,
free water,
Coolidge,
North Chavez,
Iyanbito, a Shell Oil Co. Refinery, bless it,
        west, west going, you see
        red gods emerging out of the cliffs
        couple miles north of the AT&SF railroad,
keep going and next you're by
Wingate Army Depot, ammo storage,
up on the hills rows & rows, bunkers
of ammo stashed, freight cars pull away
loaded for war, for Vietcong,
        west, whooosh, a Cadillac,
        fat white cat and blonde teenybopper,
        hi baby shove it,
Church Rock turnoff, an Indian man waits,
we stop for him and he hurries to us,

Where you headed?
Gallup.
Okay.
> West, California is too far,
> once I been to California, got lost
> in L. A., got laid in Fresno,
> got jailed in Oakland, got fired in Barstow,
> and came home,

Gallup, Indian Capital of The World, shit,
the heat is impossible, the cops wear riot helmets,
.38s and smirks, you better not get into trouble
and you better not be Indian, bail's low though,
Indian Ceremonial Aug. 7–10, traders bring cashboxes,
bars standing room only and have bouncers who are mean
wear white hats and white.

> West, sometimes I feel like going on.
> West towards the sun in the evening.

THE URBAN INDIANS

Approximately half of the Indians counted by the 1970 census lived in urban areas—400,000 of 800,000. In the city—there are sizable Indian populations in Los Angeles, San Francisco, Denver, Phoenix, Albuquerque, Omaha, Minneapolis, and Chicago—the rural tribesman has to find a "home." His foray into suburbia has its ironic difficulties ("The Indian in Suburbia," by Wamblee Wastee, *The American Indian*, San Francisco Indian Center, March, 1964, p. 3). But, once he has settled, the city Indian often joins with people of other tribes to establish an urban tribalism ("Urban Indians Reconquer Their Urban Center," *Talking Leaf*, Los Angeles Indian Center, Feb., 1969, p. 3.)

The Indian in Suburbia

by Wamblee Wastee

Suburbia is a word used which means in the outlying parts of a city. Here in the Bay Area an Indian can live in the heart of a city and still be in suburbia.

When an Indian family first arrives in either Oakland or San Francisco, they will find thousands of cement streets running in every direction. On these streets will be tens of thousand automobiles. These automobiles are filled with people who are trying to kill each other off with these steel monsters almost as fast as the white man killed off the buffalo. To find his way around in this cement prairie the white man uses a map, and so must the Indian. Reading a map is not easy at best. All names will be strange and signs are not on every corner. A street will go along for a mile, and then suddenly there will be a big building, lake, park. Maybe one or two miles later the street starts again.

All of the houses have numbers and some of the streets are called by numbers. Some streets have other names and in many cases streets are not called streets but Avenues, Places, Boulevards, and Freeways. Of these, Freeways are the most dangerous and no one walks on them. Sometimes it is even hard to drive on them, and the reason for these Freeways is so that the people who work in the city can get to other cities fast without going thru a city. There is even one Freeway in San Francisco which very few people use and it really doesn't go anywhere but it's there.

This may sound confusing to some of our people on the reservations who have never been to California, but it is. So if you are planning a trip out, thinking of relocating or have applied for relocation, in all cases have the relocation officer or someone show you how to read a map and what all the

markings mean. Then go over it again and again. If you do
this you will be one step ahead of those of us who came out
here before you.

Urban Indians Reconquer Their Urban Center

Latest word from the Intertribal Friendship House in Oakland is that there has been quite a change made in the all-
over organizational set-up.

Seems that after too many moons, the Indians have taken
over the command of the entire organization, much to the
outspoken displeasure of "former" non-Indian friends.

It is a pity that these former friends are upset, but this is
going on all over, as more and more our people are demanding Indians in control of Indian organizations.

Future "friends" will simply have to understand that we
wear feathers, BUT only sometimes; and even then we are
quite able to "run" the show.

Our friends simply have to realize that we wish to be
friends, but ANY native American Indian organization must
be under complete Indian control; otherwise it is simply not
an Indian organization.

In short: Come share with us, but on our terms.

TODAY YOUNG INDIANS
MUST RELINQUISH THEIR CUSTOMS
by Richard St. Germaine

The frustration and bitterness of Indian youth who are
taught they must emulate the white man to be accepted and successful is poignantly expressed in the

words of a Wisconsin teenager of the Lac Courte
Oreille tribe. In commenting on his own words a few
years later, the young Indian wrote: "Four years have
passed and my philosophy has changed immensely.
Since that time I have graduated from college, taught
school, sat on Alcatraz, and am now returning to graduate school. Education is indeed important to our people, but it no longer seems necessary to 'relinquish our
customs.' " . . . ("Today Young Indians Must Relinquish Their Customs," by Richard St. Germaine, *Wisconsin Indian Youth Council Newsletter,* Vol. V, No. 2,
March, 1967, pp. 3–4.)

The purpose of my composition is not intended to offend
anyone. I am merely expressing my ideas toward how the
young Indian should get ahead today. I feel my theme is
direct and hits on my subject inadequately. The startling
and over-dramatic headline was a technique for attracting
attention.

The young Indian today is being taken advantage of con-
tinually. Malefactors are fellow white classmates and co-
workers. Prejudice looms around every corner in a white
world. My best friends are white and I can talk openly with
them about the Indians' problems. *Yet, even my best friends
have at one time or other inadvertently cracked jokes or
made other remarks concerning the Indians' plight.* Big shots
and young high society groups snub their noses at the color
of brown skin or, for that matter, any color other than
white.

Some administrators take advantage of the Indian. I, myself, have gone through this treatment and witnessed other
cases. I have heard supposedly mature men (church-going
and respected in their communities) slander and hurl other
defamatory remarks toward the Indians. I have watched Indians utterly bow down to public officials.

Society as a whole has stereotyped the Indian race as one: uneducated, remote, and low-classed. They degrade us unhesitatingly. And, now, it is time for us to prove them wrong and advance, instead of declining.

To get ahead nowadays, a young Indian must be respected, intelligent, educated, and AGGRESSIVE. These are traits of some of the white men who surge above the Indian. In order to fully ascend to the white man's level, the Indian must set aside his bow and arrow, his feathers and drums— his diehard customs—for a time. Recently, I spoke with an elderly friend of mine, a leader of a strong Indian clan from my reservation, a wise and respected man, an Indian. He realized that the young Indians who do gain a well-deserved education usually leave the reservation and gain respected names for themselves among the white people. Potential leaders have been lost in this manner from the reservation. But, there are a few who remain with their people. I take my hat off to these few . . . they are worthful examples of the Indian of tomorrow. At the same time, I also dedicate a line to those educated Indians who left. Of the future— sooner than watch the Indian sink down to the lowest level of the social category, desperately clinging to their old customs, I would rather see them accept more of the white man's trends and build in intelligence. This intelligence will certainly rub off on their children.

Do not get the impression that I urge the young Indian to leave his traditions entirely behind him. After he educates himself in a white world, if he comes back, this is great. I do not dislike the Indian ways. I myself Indian-danced for over five years as a youngster, and, now, could no more think of giving up my two costumes than my right arm. My closest friend, nearly a brother to me, is an Indian. My whole family is Indian. I only mean that an Indian should first educate himself and socialize with the white world, setting aside his old customs while doing so . . . then decide which path he shall take.

CHANGING CULTURES

by Howard Rock

> Alaska has been called "the last hope" of government Indian policy. In the Eskimo, Aleut, and Athapascan villages, the land claims of the natives and the oil boom on the North Slope offer the final confrontation of aboriginal rights *vs.* technological exploitation. The effect of urban life, the mass media, and the white man's culture upon the ancient and cohesive traditional life style of the Eskimos is lamented by an Alaskan native writer Howard Rock. ("Changing Cultures," Fairbanks, Alaska, *Tundra Times*, Vol. I, No. 4, Nov. 19, 1962.)

There is a silent struggle that is going on in northern Alaska that most people are not aware of. It may not seem to be a serious thing to most people, but to the natives, who are enmeshed in it, it is a serious thing, indeed.

The struggle is the interchanging of two cultures. One is the relentlessly driving modern civilization and the other is the ancient, the so-called primitive culture.

Up to now it would seem to be an uneven struggle, and in many aspects it is.

What makes it unique is that the ancient culture is resisting the onslaught of civilization on some facets of its complex nature.

In the case of the Arctic people, it is a well-known fact that they do not feel civilization is adverse altogether. They have accepted many of the fine things civilization has had to offer.

On the other hand they, the Eskimos especially, are resisting those things that seek to undermine their culture.

Unfortunately, some religious denominations frown upon Eskimo dancing.

The Eskimos are puzzled why the dance is frowned upon, especially after scrutinizing some of the provocative civilized dances. This makes them feel that some parsons should divert their frowns toward the dances their civilization tolerates.

Unfortunately, though, some parsons have been successful in prohibiting the Eskimo dance, leaving a void, and not offering anything to take its place.

To take the dance away from the Eskimo is to take some of his spiritual being. In conversion he may be purer, perhaps, but he is out of his natural self. To coin a word—he is no longer himself. He is detached from one of the accustomed facets of his culture.

The Eskimo dance is but one example. There are other facets that would fall in the same category—whaling, ancient celebrations, foods, hunting and fishing, and dog-teams.

Eskimos, having been exposed to civilization for some eighty years, which is a very short time as history goes, have learned to like good things of civilization.

In liking them, they have blended them into their culture and made them work harmoniously. But, in the process, problems have arisen. These can be solved, the Eskimos believe, by mutual assistance between their culture and that of civilization.

Semi-cash-economy has come to be one of the problems. Jet-age acceleration of civilization has bypassed many natives of Alaska and left them with little means of keeping up with the pace.

Educational standards in native areas have likewise been bypassed by the rush of civilization. Roads have been bypassed by airplanes.

These things need not have happened if any of the Appropriations Committees in Washington, D.C., had tended to their own backyard, instead of furnishing graft money to Vietnam, Yugoslavia, and other such countries.

In getting back to the merging of the two cultures in northern Alaska and the problems created by them, it is the opinion of the *Tundra Times* that studies be made of this unusual problem, studies that would probe the compatability of the two cultures.

The studies should be made at high levels and by unbiased participants.

Perhaps the results of such a study may lead to a solution that may create a happy blending of the two cultures, and alleviate the pressure for the citizens of the north.

CIVIL RIGHTS AND INDIAN RIGHTS

by Sam Kolb

In a magazine cartoon of a few years ago, an aged Indian, in a blanket, skeptically told a young black, in modish clothes: "I hope your Martin Luther King, Jr., proves to be more effective than our Sitting Bull." Recently, young Indians have sharply differentiated between civil rights, for blacks, and treaty rights, for Indians, although they recognize the affinity among differing minorities for "human rights." ("As I See It," by Sam Kolb, *Talking Leaf*, Vol. III, No. 1, Feb. 15, 1968, p. 3.)

I have noted with increased interest the efforts of other minorities to enlist the support and participation of the American Indian to assist them in civil rights demonstrations and civil disobedience.

The Indian is independent and always has been. He is one of the few groups who has undertaken his own betterment in an uncomplaining and constructive manner. I think it would detract from his role if he took part in any demonstrations.

Martin Luther King, in particular, has cited efforts to enlist Indians in an upcoming civil disobedience demonstration. Possibly we could participate if these drives were aimed at the solution of Indian problems *first*. As it is, I suspect that the support of the American Indian is being courted to cash in on the overwhelming public sympathy which the American people have for the Indian and his problem. Maybe they should create a NAACPAIL, National Association for the Advancement of Colored People *And Indians Later!*

I think the Indian has it within his power to *solve his own problems*, using his own methods.

ON THE ART OF STEALING HUMAN RIGHTS
by Jerry Gambill

In the Virginia Colony, the earliest laws prohibiting intermarriage between whites and non-whites were directed against Indians, not blacks. Since the 1600's, the legal and social acts of discrimination originally established to exclude Indians have served as the basis for many racist practices facing newer minorities. Jerry Gambill, a Mohawk scholar, and editor of *Akwesasne Notes*, outlines the methodology of making an

Indian a "non-person." (Speech by Jerry Gambill, at a conference on human rights at Tobique Reserve in New Brunswick, Aug., 1968, printed in *Akwesasne Notes*, Vol. I, No. 7, July, 1969.)

Methods must coincide with the type of problem and, in the case of human rights, the reception or resistance which the majority have toward your aims. The Indian has problems peculiar to *Indians alone* and deals with a very receptive society.

The Indian's problem in solution has much of its roots in a lack of communication. As soon as the Indians become articulate enough as a people, and signs indicate they are fast becoming that way, their aims will become clear and society will become receptive to our wants.

One fact is clear to the Indian. He does not go where he is not wanted. You can't force people to accept you. Nothing is ever gained by anything destructive. At least, if acceptance is what you are seeking.

The Indian's interests are locked within himself, his proud past, his country, and his own destiny as shaped by himself.

Being other than white isn't common cause enough to justify civil disobedience.

The art of denying Indians their human rights has been refined to a science. The following list of commonly used techniques will be helpful in "burglar-proofing" your reserves and *your rights.*

GAIN THE INDIANS' CO-OPERATION—It is much easier to steal someone's human rights if you can do it with his OWN co-operation.

SO. . . .

1. Make him a non-person. Human rights are for people. Convince Indians their ancestors were savages, that they were pagan, that Indians are drunkards. Make them wards

of the government. Make a legal distinction, as in the Indian Act, between Indians and persons. Write history books that tell half the story.

2. Convince the Indian that he should be patient, that these things take time. Tell him that we are making progress, and that progress takes time.

3. Make him believe that things are being done for his own good. Tell him that you're sure that after he has experienced your laws and actions that he will realize how good they have been. Tell the Indian he has to take a little of the bad in order to enjoy the benefits you are conferring on him.

4. Get some Indian people to do the dirty work. There are always those who will act for you to the disadvantage of their own people. Just give them a little honor and praise. This is generally the function of band councils, chiefs, and advisory councils: They have little legal power, but can handle the tough decisions such as welfare, allocation of housing, etc.

5. Consult the Indian, but do not act on the basis of what you hear. Tell the Indian he has a voice and go through the motions of listening. Then interpret what you have heard to suit your own needs.

6. Insist that the Indian "GOES THROUGH THE PROPER CHANNELS." Make the channels and the procedures so difficult that he won't bother to do anything. When he discovers what the proper channels are and becomes proficient at the procedures, change them.

7. Make the Indian believe that you are working hard for him, putting in much overtime and at a great sacrifice, and imply that he should be appreciative. This is the ultimate in skills in stealing human rights: When you obtain the thanks of your victim.

8. Allow a few individuals to "MAKE THE GRADE" and then point to them as examples. Say that the "HARDWORK-

ERS" and the "GOOD" Indians have made it, and that therefore it is a person's own fault if he doesn't succeed.

9. Appeal to the Indian's sense of fairness, and tell him
that, even though things are pretty bad, it is not right for
him to make strong protests. Keep the argument going on
his form of protest and avoid talking about the real issue.
Refuse to deal with him while he is protesting. Take all the
fire out of his efforts.

10. Encourage the Indian to take his case to court. This is
very expensive, takes lots of time and energy, and is very
safe because the laws are stacked against him. The court's
ruling will defeat the Indian's cause, but makes him think he
has obtained justice.

11. Make the Indian believe that things could be worse,
and that, instead of complaining about the loss of human
rights, to be grateful for the human rights we do have. In
fact, convince him that to attempt to regain a right he has
lost is likely to jeopardize the rights that he still has.

12. Set yourself up as the protector of the Indian's human
rights, and then you can choose to act on only those violations you wish to act upon. By getting successful action on a
few minor violations of human rights, you can point to these
as examples of your devotion to his cause. The burglar who
is also the doorman is the perfect combination.

13. Pretend that the reason for the loss of human rights is
for some other reason than that the person is an Indian. Tell
him some of your best friends are Indians, and that his loss
of rights is because of his housekeeping, his drinking, his
clothing. If he improves in these areas, it will be necessary
for you to adopt another technique of stealing his rights.

14. Make the situation more complicated than is necessary. Tell the Indian you will have to take a survey to find
out just how many other Indians are being discriminated

against. Hire a group of professors to make a year-long research project.

15. Insist on unanimity. Let the Indian know that when all the Indians in Canada can make up their minds about just what they want as a group, then you will act. Play one group's special situation against another group's wishes.

16. Select very limited alternatives, neither of which has much merit, and then tell the Indian that he indeed has a choice. Ask, for instance, if he could or would rather have council elections in June or December, instead of asking if he wants them at all.

17. Convince the Indian that the leaders who are the most beneficial and powerful are dangerous and not to be trusted. Or simply lock them up on some charge like driving with no lights. Or refuse to listen to the real leaders and spend much time with the weak ones. Keep the people split from their leaders by sowing rumor. Attempt to get the best leaders into high-paying jobs where they have to keep quiet to keep their paycheck coming in.

18. Speak of the common good. Tell the Indian that you can't consider yourselves when there is the whole nation to think of. Tell him that he can't think only of himself. For instance, in regard to hunting rights, tell him we have to think of all the hunters, or the sporting-goods industry.

19. Remove rights so gradually that people don't realize what has happened until it is too late. Again, in regard to hunting rights, first restrict the geographical area where hunting is permitted, then cut the season to certain times of the year, then cut the limits down gradually, then insist on licensing, and then Indians will be on the same grounds as white sportsmen.

20. Rely on reason and logic (your reason and logic) instead of rightness and morality. Give thousands of reasons

for things, but do not get trapped into arguments about what is right.

21. Hold a conference on HUMAN RIGHTS, have everyone blow off steam and tension, and go home feeling that things are well in hand.

THE NEW INDIAN WARS

by Mel Thom

> "The New Indian Wars" were begun on August 10, 1960, by a group of young, outspoken, university-educated Indians who founded the National Indian Youth Council. Mel Thom, a Paiute youth and aeronautics engineer, was the first president. He has since become tribal chairman of the Walker River Paiute Reservation in Nevada. ("The New Indian Wars," *American Aborigine*, National Indian Youth Council, Vol. III, No. 1, pp. 2–8.)

Indian War 1963

Let us take a look around our great country and see whom or what the Red Man of today is fighting. There definitely is a battle going on, no question about that. Indian life is steadily being destroyed. This is not a fictitious "fight-nothing" like that on TV and in the movies. One similarity though, the Indian is losing. Indian life has been threatened ever since the white man came upon the shores of this land, and the threat continues today. It's a confused fight involving a great amount of misunderstanding. The misunderstanding is growing worse because there is little or no understanding of the Indian's side.

This is a different kind of war—a cold war, one might say. It's a struggle against destructive forces the Indian cannot sometimes even see, let alone understand. But he knows that these forces exist, for the results are evident. Indians die at an early age. Indian social structure is torn apart. Indians are poor considering what it takes to provide a decent living in this day. There is no question about what these destructive forces are doing. Sometimes these destructive forces are even disguised as progress.

Strangely enough, the Indian has a good defense, if he were allowed to use a defense. His defense, which can also be an offense, is the fact that he is the original American. His life is rooted in all of this great country. The rights to his lands existed long before and subsequent to America. The American government legally obligated itself to protect the life of the original inhabitants and give general assistance.

The weakest link in the Indian's defense is his lack of understanding of this modern-type war. Indians have not been able to use political action, propaganda, and power as well as their opponents. The enemy has made notable gains; they have deployed their forces well. Enemy forces have successfully scattered Indian people and got them divided against themselves.

So, on came the forces of "friends and experts"—while we sit back—waiting for answers to our "problems." They introduced us to a new phrase—"Indian problems." They even created a new field of study and mechanics for themselves. Now, we ask ourselves, have our experts given us any answers that mean anything—or, is the job really our own? For many years now, a small number of Indians have been talking about our plight. We ask ourselves a lot of questions —"What can we do?"—"Where do we begin?"—"Are we doomed to lose our lands and rights?"—"Can we rally our own people to stand together and realize their plight?"—"Is there still enough 'fight' left in Indian blood to protect our heritage and rights?"

At first, we found ourselves parroting the words of Indian experts. This didn't do anyone much good. We spoke from our mouths only—not from our hearts. We received encouraging words from tribal leaders, but many of them were part of a tribal faction and did not have ambitions of real unity. The strongest unity seems to lie with the younger people. So, it is here that we must build that unity.

The struggle for Indian causes must be carried forward with Indians at the controls—and only by arousing more sincere interest and concern can we hope to fight forward for the Indian cause—and build a greater Indian America.

Indian War 1964

The opposition to Indians is a monstrosity which cannot be beaten by any single action, unless we as Indian people could literally rise up in unison and take what is ours by force. We see, however, that our Indian force is small, confused, and regretfully does not include all of our Indian people. Last year, we were onlookers; this year, we got into some small campaigns. We now speak with some experience.

We are convinced, more than ever before, that this is real war. Indian life is steadily torn apart and Indian integrity is downgraded—all from within a legal framework. Our opposition is out to destroy Indians as a people. It is becoming more obvious that our opposition is the present American system that deals with American Indians. We are told that we must quit being like Indians because it is wrong to have strong and real cultural ties in this "modern progressive world." Action and policies have been enacted by our governing powers to take away Indian land, break up Indian communities, disregard solemn treaties and agreements, force a system of values upon Indian people, and destroy any hope that Indians can exist as a people. All this is being done without even touching the conscience of our American system.

Our great country actually has the gall to tell us that they are helping us to a better way of life, and that we do not have the basic ability to know what is best for ourselves. While it is true that Indian people have lost faith in fellow Indians to take unilateral action, no people in this world have ever been exterminated without putting up a last resistance. Citizens of this country talk of the Indian that "used to be," and of the "vanishing American." They do not completely realize that we still exist, and that we still have the same basic hopes for life that our forefathers did.

The white man does not treat us as his own kind, and Indians are appalled at the way he treats other white men. The white man has ignored treaties and agreements and continues to force jurisdiction on Indian nations without asking consent. We are looked down upon as backward people and the assumption is made that we must become like the white man to find peace of mind. No one ever asked us what we wanted. There is always someone ready to put words in our mouths.

The more we think about our situation and the more we learned how it developed, we wonder how we could have endured such treatment. Awareness to our situation has brought out anger, and, with anger and concern, "hope" is born.

So far, in our modern war, Indians have not done so badly. Some Indian people have retreated and isolated themselves from the rest of the world. This is a wise move with the threat of cultural extermination. A sad note is that many Indians have been destroying themselves with the poisons of the dominant society. We are becoming increasingly aware of these poisons which have eaten away at Indian

ranks for the past century and a half. These poisons are
greed, abuse of power, distrust, and no respect for any people who are a little different.

Up to this point it has been the old people who have kept
the Indian hope alive. As in the case with any campaign involving lives, the younger people are called upon to carry on
active fighting. Younger Indians are responding to this call
and more will join in, once they become aware. Indian
youth councils have been organized on college campuses
throughout the country. The National Indian Youth Council
set up a protest against the encroachment on treaty rights.
Younger Indians are taking more leadership responsibilities
in their home communities. The policies of our government
and helping agencies have been to take young Indians away
from their homes in order to "improve them." They are told
to go back and change their backward people. Young Indians are told to join in on this great civilizing venture. Ironi-
cally, this is the same tactic used by the U.S. Army in using
Indian scouts to wipe out Indian resistance in historical
times. Little by little, we are more able to identify our present-day "renegades" and rid them from our leadership
ranks.

The tactic base used by Indians is to hit strategically at
our opposition. We are small in numbers, and we must make
every effort count. We must know our opposition's motives
and means of working against us. In other words, we must
have a full understanding of the present American system
that deals with Indians. We must know the forces that make
changes in that system, and we must know how to use the
forces that make changes. We must know the political
forces, communication media, and social structure which
make up this country. Without this basic knowledge, our
efforts can be easily sidetracked and wasted effort exerted.
Our opposition is a great monster that threatens to absorb

us, to render us voiceless and take away our recognition as Indian people. We know that the odds are against us, but we also realize that we are fighting for the lives of future Indian generations.

There is a conference table to talk out differences and reach agreements. But, to Indians, this is a concession table rather than a conference table.

Indians are not politically powerful enough to enforce their agreements. You see, besides making agreements, it's the American way to infringe upon the less powerful party of an agreement. Agreements between Indian tribes and this country, as we very well know, can be broken whenever this country chooses. Rather than talk with respect to Indians, we are offered a few dollars which are supposed to keep us happy and quiet.

There is increased activity over on the Indian side. There are disagreements, laughing, singing, outbursts of anger, and occasionally some planning. Given some time, it looks like an effort can be put forth. Indians are gaining confidence and courage that their cause is right.

The struggle goes on. We know more about what we stand to lose. We know more about how this modern system works. Indians are gathering together to deliberate their destiny. We want to talk about what is wrong and what needs to be done. We are concerned about what the future holds for Indian people. This is encouraging.

If we can hold our ranks together, our chances of gaining in our modern campaign are good. There is growing hope. We will continue to work for a Greater Indian America.

CHANGES

by Clyde Warrior

Of all the new Indian leaders who have risen to national prominence in the "Red Power" movement, the
most legendary is the late Clyde Warrior, who died in
1969. A Ponca of Oklahoma, his writings and speeches
have been reprinted in tribal and student publications
throughout the country. His widest-known work is
"Which One Are You? Five Types of Young Indians"
(pamphlet, *Clyde Warrior Institute in American Indian Studies*, undated). His philosophy of social change
is expressed in "This Indian Revolution." (Quoted in
The New Indians, by Stan Steiner, New York, Harper
& Row, 1968, pp. 70–2.)

Which One Are You?
Five Types of Young Indians

Among American Indian youth today there exists a rather
pathetic scene, in fact, a very sick, sad, sorry scene. This
scene consists of the various types of Indian students found
in various institutions of learning throughout American society. It is very sad that these institutions, and whatever con-
ditioning takes place, create these types. For these types are
just what they are, types, and not full, real human beings, or
people.

Many of you probably already know these types. Many of
you probably know the reasons why these types exist. This
writer does not pretend to know why. This writer can only
offer an opinion as to names and types, define their characteristics, and offer a possible alternative; notice alternative
—not a definite solution. All this writer is merely saying is

he does not like Indian youth being turned into something that is not real, and that somebody needs to offer a better alternative.

Type A—SLOB or HOOD. This is the individual who receives his definition of self from the dominant society, and, unfortunately, sees this kind in his daily relationships and associations with his own kind. Thus, he becomes this type by dropping out of school, becomes a wino, steals, eventually becomes a court case, and is usually sent off. If lucky, he marries, mistreats his family, and becomes a real pain to his tribal community as he attempts to cram that definition [of himself] down the society's throat. In doing this, he becomes a Super-Slob. Another Indian hits the dust through no fault of his own.

Type B—JOKER. This type has defined himself that to be an Indian is a joke. An Indian does stupid, funny things. After defining himself, from cues society gave him, he proceeds to act as such. Sometimes he accidentally goofs-up, sometimes unconsciously on purpose, after which he laughs, and usually says, "Well, that's Indian." And he goes through life a bungling clown.

Type C—REDSKIN "WHITE-NOSER" or THE SELL-OUT. This type has accepted and sold out to the dominant society. He has accepted that definition that anything Indian is dumb, usually filthy, and immoral, and to avoid this is to become a "LITTLE BROWN AMERICAN" by associating with everything that is white. He may mingle with Indians, but only when it is to his advantage, and not a second longer than is necessary. Thus, society has created the fink of finks.

Type D—ULTRA-PSEUDO-INDIAN. This type is proud that he is Indian, but for some reason does not know how one acts. Therefore he takes his cues from non-Indian sources, books, shows, etc., and proceeds to act "Indian." With each action, which is phony, we have a person becoming unconsciously phonier and phonier. Hence, we have a proud, phony Indian.

Type E—ANGRY NATIONALIST. Although abstract and ideological, this type is generally closer to true Indianness than the other types, and he resents the others for being ashamed of their own kind. Also, this type tends to dislike the older generation for being "Uncle Tomahawks" and "yes-men" to the Bureau of Indian Affairs and whites in general. The "Angry Nationalist" wants to stop the current trend toward personality disappearance, and institute changes that will bring Indians into contemporary society as real human beings; but he views this, and other problems, with bitter abstract and ideological thinking. For thinking this [he] is termed radical, and [he] tends to alienate himself from the general masses of Indians, for speaking what appears, to him, to be truths.

None of these types is the ideal Indian. . . .

It appears that what is needed is genuine contemporary creative thinking, democratic leadership to set guidelines, cues, and goals for the average Indian. The guidelines and cues have to be *based on true Indian philosophy geared to modern times*. This will not come about without nationalistic pride in one's self and one's own kind.

This group can evolve only from today's college youth. Not from those who are ashamed, or those who have sold out, or those who do not understand true Indianism. Only from those with pride and love and understanding of the People and the People's ways from which they come can this evolve. And this appears to be the major task of the National Indian Youth Council—for, without a people, how can one have a cause?

This writer says this because he is fed up with religious workers and educationalists incapable of understanding, and pseudo-social scientists who are consciously creating social and cultural genocide among American Indian youth.

I am fed up with bureaucrats who try to pass off "rules and regulations" for organizational programs that will bring progress.

I am sick and tired of seeing my elders stripped of dignity and low rated in the eyes of their young.

I am disturbed to the point of screaming when I see American Indian youth accepting the horror of "American conformity," as being the only way for Indian progress. While those who do not join the great American mainstream of personalityless neurotics are regarded as "incompetents and problems."

The National Indian Youth Council must introduce to this sick room of stench and anonymity some fresh air of new Indianness. A fresh air of new honesty and integrity, a fresh air of new Indian realism, a fresh air of a new Greater Indian America.

How about it? Let's raise some hell!

This Indian Revolution

I believe what is at the heart of this Indian revolution is bureaucracy out of control, over-institutions, alienation of individuals, exploitation of people—our friends and neighbors. And the Indian suffers these things more than most people. He is the worst victim. But the powers-that-be look at these people they say it's all their fault: What they should do is "get educated," or "they don't have any morals," or they're "racially inferior." Which doesn't mean nothing. It only justifies their being.

And American Indians are fed up with this. They know that's not the problem. They know it's the system: The social, political, economic structure of this country is such that it causes these things. And we Indians are beginning to see that the only way to change it is to destroy it. And to build something else.

And this isn't unique, this type of thinking, to Indians. This is what the students at Berkeley are mad about. There's not that much difference in their thinking, or their anger. This is what people are screaming about in Vietnam. This is what Fulbright says, and Morse: that maybe we should stop and re-evaluate ourselves as a person, as a group of people, as a community, as a nation. And see what we're doing not only to each other but to ourselves.

Is this an American way of hollowing out the insides of people?

And, as I see it, before we change, things are going to get worse. There are going to be more riots. And if it doesn't change, then the students and the Indians might just smash it, and change it themselves. These people are going to get so angry, so mad, that they're going to destroy the American society, without any thought of what to replace it with.

If American society is so goddamn great, then how come it creates social movements like this? If everything is really ducky, then how come we have things like this happening? Maybe we're not those good, pious people we project to the world; maybe we, as Americans, are really bastards. If America is so good, if America is so great, if America is so charitable, then why are we forcing people to behave like this? Why are we warping and twisting them to where the only thing they can do is come out with volcanic eruptions of violence?

Can it be, perhaps, that we are wrong?

How long will Indians tolerate this? Negroes, Mexican

Americans, and Puerto Ricans could only take colonialism, exploitation, and abuse for so long; then they did something about it. Will American Indians wait until their reservations and lands are eroded away, and they are forced into urban ghettos, before they start raising hell with their oppressors?

▲▲▲▲▲▲▲▲▲▲▲▲▲▲▲▲▲▲▲▲▲▲▲▲▲

IV. MY TEACHER IS A LIZARD: EDUCATION AND CULTURE

YOU ARE HIGHLY EDUCATED—
THAT DOES NOT HELP US ANY AT ALL

by Albert Attocknie, Chief, Comanche tribe

"The White Man is a barbarian. He rejects his Mother
—the Earth," said a Sioux philosopher in the nineteenth century. At the first convention of the National
Congress of American Indians, held near the end of
World War II (1944), the ancient trepidation was directed not against the white man, but toward the
"young, educated Indians." The old medicine man and
chief of the Comanche tribe, Attocknie, who spoke of
this paradox, was the only delegate given a standing
ovation, according to the convention minutes. ("Minutes of the First Convention of the National Congress
of American Indians," Denver, Col., Nov. 15–18, 1944,
mimeographed paper.)

I am ignorant, but I have the interest of the young and educated Indians at heart. I came here following the young men
from my jurisdiction. I came here especially to see the
young and educated Indians organize to help the Indian
people. I hope that when you young educated Indians take
up this question of organizing for the benefit of the Indians,
you will remember that the Indians are from different
classes. There are Indians like myself who are not educated,
who are restricted, and who cannot exist under condi-

tions that will work well with the young and the educated Indians.

In the Comanche custom, young people are referred to as sons and daughters, so I want to say a few words along that line. Attempts have been made to take away the guardianship of the Indian Bureau over Indian land. I am opposed to that; and the reasons given for lifting the guardianship of the Indian Bureau from the Indians, especially to aid the uneducated Indians, is not fair. There is no reason given why that should be fair. Now, we are very proud of you, our children, that are so highly educated. Your oratory here is about as good as I have ever heard anywhere, including the halls of Congress. You are able Indians, but the advancement and achievement obtained by you educated Indians does not help us old folks any longer. Our status as Indians remains just the same. You are highly educated—that does not help us any at all. My boy's status does not save my status as an Indian, as a ward of the Government.

I want you to take this resolution that was offered here by the Chairman and insert therein words and language that will help the old Indians like myself. In Oklahoma, the old Indians are the minority. The young people have such a great majority that we never have any chance to put in the bylaws rules that we want, because the young and educated people have such a big majority that they rule us out. I would not be here if it was left to the majority. We do not question the legality of majority rule, but it is not fair. The leadership of the council is given to the young, well-educated people in my jurisdiction, a lot of them landless. Those young men really are not interested in an allotted Indian's lands or problems. That is not fair. We don't want to have control of the young, educated Indians, but we want to be represented and be given equal representation in the council affairs and before the Indian Bureau and Congress.

We can't do it under the present system, which is legal but is not fair. Now, I live on a farm. Suppose somebody quits farming, leaves the farm, and goes away somewhere, and then tells how that farm should be carried on. It is just as fair as that the younger and disinterested Indians rule the tribes. I think it is very much the same in other tribes in other states. I have been talking for a number of years. Some of you come from closed reservations, but you people who have allotted lands will understand what I mean.

It will not be long before the old Indian will be out of sight. I wish to ask you young and educated Indians to consider this resolution carefully for the older Indians' benefits. The Indian Bureau should be retained for the protection of the aged and allotted landowners. At least for a while, because the old man standing before you will, before long, pass on to follow my fathers, your fathers, and your mothers to that Happy Hunting Ground in the realms of the mysterious hereafter. I thank you.

PROTECTION AGAINST "THINKERS"— A CHEROKEE CHANT

by Jack F. and Anna G. Kilpatrick

In the tribal way, "knowing" was to be in harmony and at peace with oneself and nature, while "thinking" implied disharmony and evil. To their tribesmen, as these Cherokee writers illustrate, the "thinker" was someone who harbored "malign emotions," for he created "human disharmony with Nature." It was this cosmic concept of ecology that tribal man always "knew," modern man is still "thinking about." (*Run Toward the Nightland: Magic of the Oklahoma Chero-*

kees, by Jack F. and Anna G. Kilpatrick, Dallas, Tex., Southern Methodist University Press, pp. 170–1.)

The Cherokees conceive of most evil as being the result of human disharmony with Nature. Most of the interruption, or diversion, of the normal flow of natural forces they hypothesize as stemming from the nurturing by an individual of destructive emotions that exude an evil influence and achieve harmful results without the necessity of any implementing action.

The harboring of malign emotions is known in Cherokee religio-medicine by the circumlocutory term "thinking." The verb stem -*el*- actually has more of the force of "believing" than of "thinking": *ane:li:sgi* ["those who think"], therefore, are individuals who project evil toward other human beings by the power of thought.

Idi:gawe:sdi [holy medicines] for the purpose of protecting oneself from *ane:li:sgi* are rather numerous, and they are likely to be strewn with passages of noble beauty. The knowledge of them is confined almost exclusively to the *dida:hnvwi:sg(i)* [holy medicine people], who use them to "remake" tobacco [make it holy] for clients who blow its smoke upon themselves.

This one is for "remaking" tobacco in the usual manner:

> Now! Listen! Blue Man!
> *Ha!* Very quickly they have just come to live with You!
> *Ha,* then! They will be living with You everywhere.
> Immediately devour all their evil souls! *Ya!*
>
> Now! Listen! Yellow Man!
>
> Now! Listen! Black Man!

TOO MANY SCIENTISTS AND NOT ENOUGH CHIEFS

by Howard Rock, Tundra Times

"A warrior killed in battle could always go to the Happy Hunting Ground. But where does an Indian laid low by an anthro[pologist] go? To the library?" asks Vine Deloria, Jr., in *Custer Died for Your Sins* (New York, Macmillan, 1969). For years, tribes were polite to anthropologists, and other "ologists," who studied them, understood them, and often spoke for them. Now, the angry reaction of Indians who demand the right to speak for themselves has caused the Red Lake Chippewa to bar anthropologists and has provoked editorials such as this. ("Too Many Scientists and Not Enough Chiefs," by Howard Rock, *Tundra Times,* Aug. 29, 1969.)

The highly publicized science conference at the University of Alaska this week discussed the native people and their social changes. As [with] any high-level confab, there was little room for the natives to take any appreciable part in it. Someone realized this lack, perhaps, and the conference partially redeemed itself by having some native folks take part in the audience-participation portion of it. This might be viewed as a face-saving effort by the conferees after some static developed based on a sore thumb that spelled that there were too many scientists and not enough chiefs.

Such conferences should always have a good cross-section of the people being discussed. We believe sciences developed, on peoples especially, don't always get to the bottom of things because scientists who study a race don't always reach the real depth of the philosophies of life of those they study. As far as we know, scientists, such as anthropologists, have had no working knowledge of the languages of their subjects, which are a real key to the understanding of the intricacies of life of a particular people. Man is not like a piece of stone, whoever he is. He is a complex piece of machinery or mechanism. Based on this, we believe that no foolproof evaluation of any people, especially Eskimos and other races, has been produced to date.

Under this situation, then, conferences such as the one held at the University this week should always include people being evaluated. Through this manner of doing things, scientists, especially those who delve into human behavior, can perhaps learn a lot more than they know now because there are native people who can enlighten them.

FOURTEEN STRINGS OF PURPLE WAMPUM TO WRITERS ABOUT INDIANS

> At the "First Convocation of Indian Scholars," held at Princeton University, Princeton, N.J., in March, 1970, the tribal historians and writers pleaded that "the Indian viewpoint" be heard in academe. "People are listening to the voice of the American Indian," declared the Convocation Call, written by Dr. Alfonso Ortiz, a San Juan Pueblo anthropologist teaching at Princeton. And it requested non-Indian scholars to do likewise, as does this sardonic message of the League of Six Nations of the Iroquois. (*Six Nations Pamphlets*, Akwesasne Counselor Organization, *The People*, Hogansburg, N.Y., Vol. I, No. 2, Aug., 1968.)

We hold in our hand fourteen strings of purple wampum. These we hand, one by one, to you—authors of many American history books; writers of cheap, inaccurate, unauthentic, sensational novels; and other writers of fiction who have poisoned the minds of young Americans concerning our people, the Red Race of America; to the producers of many western cowboy and Indian television programs and moving picture shows; to those Treaty-breakers who delight in dispossessing Indian Peoples by constructing dams on Indian lands in violation of sacred treaties; and to those of this, our country, who are prone to build up the glory of their ancestors on the bonds and life-blood of our Old People:

—With this first string of wampum, we take away the fog that surrounds your eyes and obstructs your view, that you may see the truth concerning our people!

—With this second string of wampum, we pull away from your imprisoned minds the cobwebs, the net that prevents you from dealing justice to our people!

—With this third piece of wampum, we cleanse your hearts of revenge, selfishness, and injustice, that you may create love instead of hate!

—With this fourth string of wampum, we wash the blood of our people from your hands, that you may know the clasp of true friendship and sincerity!

—With this fifth string of wampum, we shrink your heads down to that of normal man, we cleanse your minds of the abnormal conceit and love of self that has caused you to walk blindly among the dark people of the world.

—With this sixth string of wampum, we remove your garments of gold, silver, and greed, that you may don the apparel of generosity, hospitality, and humanity!

—With this seventh string of wampum, we remove the dirt that fills your ears so you may hear the story and truth of our people!

—With this eighth string of wampum we straighten your tongues of crookedness, that in the future you may speak the truth concerning Indian People!

—With this ninth string of wampum, we take away the

dark clouds from the face of the sun, that its rays may purify your thoughts, that you may look forward and see America, instead of backward toward Europe!

—With this tenth string of wampum, we brush away the rough stones and sticks from your path, that you may walk erect as the first American whose name you have defamed and whose country you now occupy!

—With this eleventh string of wampum, we take away from your hands your implements of destruction—guns, bombs, firewater, diseases—and place in them instead the Pipe of Friendship and Peace, that you may sow brotherly love rather than bitter hate and injustice!

—With this twelfth string of wampum, we build you a new house with many windows and no mirrors, that you may look out and see the life and purpose of your nearest neighbor, the American Indian!

—With this thirteenth string of wampum, we tear down the wall of steel and stone you have built around the TREE OF PEACE, that you may [take] shelter beneath its branches!

—With this fourteenth string of wampum we take from the hen-coop the eagle that you have imprisoned, that this noble bird may once again fly in the sky over America!

I, Te-ha-ne-to-rens, say this!

AN UNTRUE PORTRAYAL OF THE INDIANS

In his *Studies in Classic American Literature*, D. H. Lawrence wrote, "There has been all the time, in the white American soul, a dual feeling about the Indian." He is both the "noble Red Man," and yet the "savage and bloodthirsty child." These themes are evident in the protest of the Chippewa delegations to President

Taft in 1911 (*The Motion Picture World,* Feb. 17, 1911), and the more recent letter by a Lakota tribesman to a television comic ("Open Letter to [Red] Skelton," *Rosebud Sioux Herald,* Rosebud, S.D., Vol. II, No. 14).

Indians and Hollywood: An Old Script

Members of two Chippewa delegations from Minnesota and Indians from other sections have formed in an uprising against moving pictures. . . . The Indians are contemplating a call at the White House tomorrow to lay the case before President Taft and may ask for Congressional action looking to regulation of moving pictures in which they are shown.

Robby and the Redskin (1910), Selig's Western Company scenario by Hobart Bosworth and starring Hobart Bosworth. . . . A picture was shown in which a young Indian graduate of one of the non-reservation schools was the chief figure. He was shunned by the members of his tribe upon his return to them, took to drink, but was killed after a long chase. This was denounced as an untrue portrayal of the Indians.

Open Letter to Skelton

Redskin Skelton put on one of his worst TV imitations of an Indian chief last Tuesday night I've ever seen.

Red acted as a chief who had lost his marbles and did nothing but chase butterflies around.

And the Indian maiden he followed around with his tongue out. He thinks of us Indians as evil-minded people.

We Indians are being used more and more in TV commercials and comedy acts than ever before.

But always they have us playing the part of a dumb person who would trade his horse for a jug of whiskey or blow bubbles out of his peace pipe.

Just when are people going to stop condemning us, especially the comedians?

If you must imitate us, then imitate us as the proud people we are.

And stop your damn degrading us.

> Calvin Jones, Sr.
> Soldier Creek

A WORD ON INDIAN STUDIES PROGRAMS
by Alan Parker

The bumper-stickers read: "IT'S *IN* TO BE *INDIAN*." "Interest in Indians comes in cycles," declared Dr. Frederick Dockstader, curator of the Museum of the American Indian (Heye Foundation) in New York City: "Every twenty years there is a new cycle." That cycle has entered the university curriculum in the form of Indian Studies Programs, which drew this critical response from Alan Parker, an Indian college student and leader of the Organization of Native American Students (ONAS). ("Unmelted Lumps in the Melting Pot," *Akwesasne Notes*, Vol. I, No. 7, July, 1969.)

In recent years, it has become fashionable among the nation's university communities and elsewhere to be aware of minority group voices and expressed needs. We see this realization that the different minority groups have the right and even the need to affirm the distinctiveness of their identity as a positive and healthy development even though long overdue. That many school administrations and student groups are in basic mutual agreement on this issue is a starting point beyond that gap in understanding which may exist on the specifics of implementing an Indian, black, or Mexican-American Studies program.

It has been disturbing to hear university officials on campuses located in the western states speak of proposed Indian Studies programs in terms of a rehash of existing courses in anthropology and U.S. history. Too often, with a magnanimous gesture at recruiting a qualified (i.e., equipped with a Master's degree) Indian to direct the program, schools can easily avoid the difficult question of student involvement and control without which the program can become simply another academic course, not touching the lives of the students, and of little or no relation to the communities they are from. In still another vein, some schools seem to confuse black and Mexican-American needs with that of the Indians, myopically overlooking the diversity of tribal backgrounds represented by their student body. A Sioux will have only a detached interest in the history of the Navajo and the Hopi probably less in the traditions of the Blackfeet. . . .

To stress this point again, we feel that any university-based department of Indian Studies has to be meaningful and relevant, both to the students and to the surrounding communities.

THE NEW INDIANS AND THE OLD INDIANS: CULTURAL FACTORS IN THE EDUCATION OF AMERICAN INDIANS

by Robert L. Bennett

Education is the ladder, said Manuelito, the great headman of the Navajos in the nineteenth century. "The Indian is in an infinite loneliness for education," wrote a group of young Indians seeking to establish an Indian University a few years ago. Within one decade (1950–1960), Indian college students increased by nearly 300 percent. Some of the problems facing these students and the educational systems are discussed by former Commissioner of Indian Affairs, Robert L. Bennett, a member of the Oneida tribe. (Address at the celebration of Dartmouth College's 200th Anniversary, May, 1969, mimeographed paper.)

Although Indians are a very small minority in this country—the Indian population is well under a million—there is considerable new political action taking place among the Indian communities. For more than a hundred years, Indians had remained the stolid and silent prototypes of what the white man alleged they were. But, today, Indian young people have moved in upon the fronts of community action. The Indian warrior today is fighting his great battle on the social level. He has abandoned the arrow and the musket for books and public platforms.

The transition from obscurity to a conspicuous role in contemporary political affairs has not been an easy one for the new generation of Indian youth. It has been accompanied by some confusion as to goals, some hostility to the dominant society, and a great deal of defensiveness in the way Indians see themselves. These are traits that characterize many of the social activists in this country today; but, in the Indian, they are often more acute because the culture gap between Indians and other Americans is wide and deep.

There are fundamental differences, however, between Indian social action and some of the current social movements by other groups. Indian youth are motivated by the desire to *stabilize* their communities, not disrupt them; to make them more economically viable rather than more dependent upon government largesse. They are turning to the government for increasing help, but are rejecting the paternalism that was the core of the special Indian relationship for so many decades.

"We are building, not burning," is the way one youthful Indian leader puts it. It is, indeed, true. From Florida to Alaska, there is evidence that building is going on in Indian communities. Not merely construction of facilities, like homes, and schools, and water and power lines, and roads. Community spirit is building up, too. . . .

Indians understand the tremendous importance to themselves of quality education and equality of educational opportunity. The various tribes invest about $20 million annually in college scholarships; and during the past three years that I have served as Commissioner of Indian Affairs, the Bureau of Indian Affairs contributed another $10 million for higher education aid.

Even so, only about twenty percent of the Indian college age population continues schooling beyond high school, whereas the national rate exceeds forty percent. There are serious blocks to their success in school and college—financial need being one, but the culture gap being an even greater obstacle. . . .

Even while adopting the outward aspects of modern American life, Indians today, as a whole, are probably less fully attuned to the non-Indian lifeway than many of them were in the early part of the last century. Some of the eastern tribes in those days assumed with ease and great success such European culture add-ons as systematic farming and formal schooling.

Back in the days when Oklahoma was Indian territory, Indian groups operated schools and colleges that later formed the core of the state's public school system. This kind of *leadership* in education on the part of Indians has been absent for many, many years, except in individual instances. It is only now beginning to reappear, currently in the form of Indian demands for control of elementary and secondary schools serving their children. The new interest in education is prompted by a sense of frustration with the average school program that ignores the Indian cultural backgrounds.

Indians today feel threatened by the pressures now forcing total assimilation, because they fear the loss of their self-identity. Being *Indian* and being aware of it sustained them during years of oppression. They challenge the motives of those who would make them less Indian. They seek from education the ability to be both Americans *and* Indians. An either/or choice is intolerable to them. Because Indian history and Indian contributions to the building of this Nation are an integral part of our national history, Indians ask that these facts be fully acknowledged within the framework of our educational programs. . . .

The Indian's determination to retain his identity has contributed to a social phenomenon in modern America—the revival of tribalism. To be sure, today's tribalism has little in common with primitive tribalism, other than to retain remnants of the religious orientation of the Indian society. Today's tribal structures are usually modeled upon American governmental forms, and the objectives and services of tribal governments are, broadly speaking, comparable to those of county governments. The new tribalism is multi-ethnic in character, as is the Indian culture itself. Indian lifewa ·s have been modified by the Spanish horse and Spanish weaving and by the industrious, acquisitive English *mores*. They have also been modified by the trade and agricultural schools of the nineteenth and early twentieth centuries, and by commercialized farming and motorized deep-sea fishing; by World War II and the enlistment of thousands of young Indian men; by air transportation and rocketry. Native Alaskans man the defense early-warning system on the Arctic, Navajos and others assemble intricate electronic devices for space exploration, and the tribes are turning to computers to help keep account of their natural resources.

But the new Indian doesn't always feel comfortable in his new role. The tenor of Indian thinking is well expressed by a student who recently graduated from the federal Institute of American Indian Arts in Santa Fe. He composed a brief piece of poetry that is memorable to me not only because it demonstrates literary artistry but also because of its revealing undertone of bravado. It goes like this:

> We shall learn all these devices the white man has.
> We shall handle his tools for ourselves.
> We shall master his machinery and his inventions,
>   his skills, his medicine, his planning.
> But we'll retain our beauty
> And still be Indian.

Some Indians, like myself, walk always in two worlds, trying to maintain the perspective of both and to draw unto ourselves the best of both. This is not always done with ease, yet it is the course that must be walked by all American Indian children growing up today. It will be harder for them than it was for me, because the gap between the traditional Indian lifeway and the new technological society is far greater than was the gap between rural and city life in the earlier part of the century. Some of the traits and values that are the very core of contemporary American society are totally alien to their Indian upbringing. They must learn to live by the new code, yet their heritage cautions them against foolishly abandoning the basic values of the old.

EVERYONE TALKS IN POETRY

A student at the Institute of American Indian Arts, in Santa Fe, New Mexico, was praised for his poetry. He objected: *In my tribe we have no poets. Everyone talks in poetry.* If poetry is the magical use of symbols and rhythm "to make life," as the Greeks defined it, or "to remake life," as the Cherokees say, his romanticism was realistic, at least in part. For in no segment of our society are poetry and song as religiously vital as among tribal traditionalists and modernists alike, as these young Indian poets attest.

"Love Poems and Spring Poems and Dream Poems and War Poems," by Gerald Vizenor, *Anishinabe Nagamon*, Minn., Nodin Press, 1965, pp. 21, 24, 27, 41, 50, 62, 83, 84, 88.

"Snow, The Last," by Joseph Concha, *Lonely Deer: Poems by a Pueblo Boy*, Taos, N. Mex., Taos Pueblo Council, 1969.

"Grandfather and I," and "A New Visitor (To the Pueblo)," *Feathered Words*, Taos Pueblo Day School, Spring and Winter, 1969.

"In One Day My Mother Grew Old," by Courtney Moyah, *Drumbeats*, Santa Fe, N. Mex., Institute of

American Indian Arts, Vol. II, No. 5, April 3, 1969, p. 5.

"Untitled," by Vance Iron Good, and "My Life," by Jeanne Baker, *Akwesasne Notes*, Roosevelt, N.Y., Mohawk Nation, Vol. I., No. 7, July, 1969.

"The Man from Washington," by James Welch, *The American Indian Speaks*, edited by John R. Milton, Vermillion, S.D., University of South Dakota Press, 1969, p. 27.

"One Chip of Human Bone," and "Poem for Vietnam," by Ray Young Bear, *Pembroke Magazine*, N. Car., Pembroke State University, 1971.

"Three Poems," by Calvin O'John; "War Signs," by Willie George; "New Way, Old Way," by Dave Martin Nez, *The Writers' Reader*, Santa Fe, N. Mex., Institute of American Indian Arts, Spring, 1964.

"Walk Proud, Walk Straight, Let Your Thoughts Race," by Patty Harjo, p. 1, "When I Was Young, My Father Said" by Bruce Ignacio, p. 2, 1968 Sixth Annual Vincent Price Awards in Creative Writing, Santa Fe, N. Mex., Institute of American Indian Arts.

"Sorry About That," by Kenneth Kale, "Letters to the Editor," Window Rock, Az., *Navajo Times*, undated.

"Death," by Janie Bullis, p. 103, "I Am a Papago Girl," by Frances Kisto, p. 16, "It Is Not!," p. 163, *The New Trail*, The Phoenix Indian School, Az., 1953.

"Loser," by David Reeves, *The Word Passer*, Navajo Nation, Az., Vol. I, No. 3, March–April, 1969.

Love Poems and Spring Poems
and Dream Poems and War Poems

Translated from the Anishinabe by Gerald Vizenor

LOVE POEM, I

> i am thinking
> . . . nia

> i am thinking
> . . . nia

> i have found my lover
> . . . nia

> i think it is so

LOVE POEM, II

the sound of a loon
i thought

it was my lover
paddling

LOVE POEM, III

i have been waiting
a long time around the drum
for my lover

to come over
where i am sitting

SPRING POEM, I

as my eyes
look across the prairie
i feel the summer
in the spring

DREAM POEM, I

the clear sky
loves to hear me sing

DREAM POEM, II

with a large bird
above me
i am walking
in the sky

WAR POEM, I

moving forward and back
from the woodland to the prairie
dakota women
weeping
as they gather
their wounded men

the sound of their weeping
comes back to us

WAR POEM, II

all around the sky
flying
the loons
are singing

WAR POEM, III

brave warriors
where have you gone
ho kwi ho ho

Snow, the Last

by Joseph Concha

Snow comes last
for it quiets down everything.

Grandfather and I

by Joseph Concha

Grandfather and I
talk
Grandfather sings
I dance
Grandfather teaches

I learn
Grandfather dies
I cry

I wait
patiently
to see Grandfather
in the world of darkness

I miss
my
Grandfather

Patient waiting
is weighted
by loneliness
I cry and cry and cry
When
will I see him?

A New Visitor (To the Pueblo)

by Joseph Concha

So you came all the way
from Taiwan
just to be an addition
to our statues.

He who created you
did he have something in mind
when he made you?

Surely there must have been a purpose
or
was there one?

In One Day My Mother Grew Old
by Courtney Moyah

In one day my mother grew old
I walked the trail, looking down
onto the ground. In one day
my mother grew old.

I came to the end of the trail near
the river. I stopped to listen to
the flowing water. In one day
my mother grew old.

I looked at the river. I heard
waves from a river beyond sight.
The waves wanted to say something,
but went away. In one day
my mother grew old.

I walked and looked at my mother's face.
She was quiet. She was life. She
waved as I came closer and held me in
her arms until water from the river
came to my eyes.

Untitled
by Vance Iron Good

The days of spring rain awaken the earth
as one would wake a dreamer
or love a young girl
gently at first.

The Man from Washington

by James Welch

The end came easy for most of us.
Packed away in our crude beginnings
in some far corner of a flat world,
we didn't expect much more
than firewood and buffalo robes
to keep us warm. The man came down,
a slouching dwarf with rainwater eyes,
and spoke to us. He promised
that life would go on as usual,
that treaties would be signed, and everyone—
man, woman and child—would be inoculated
against a world in which we had no part,
a world of wealth, promise and fabulous disease.

One Chip of Human Bone

by Ray Young Bear

one chip of human bone

it is almost fitting
to die on railroad tracks.

i can easily understand
how they felt on their
staggered walks back.

there is something about
trains, drinking, and being
an indian with nothing to lose.

Three Poems

by Calvin O'John

I

You smiled,
I smiled,
So we're both happy,
But deep down inside
There is hatred between us.
Let's not show our inside feeling
    To one another;
    Just keep on smiling
    Until we smile away our hate.

I I

A dirt road begins at the highway
And ends at our front yard.
I walk on dirt roads,
But never will I walk on highways.

I I I

That lonesome path that leads to Nowhere
Is taking me away from this lonesome place.

It Is Not!

As told by a fifth-year group in the Special Navajo Program in 1940

The Navajo Reservation a lonesome place?
It is Not!
The skies are sunny,
Clear blue,

Or grey with rain.
Each day is gay—
In Nature's way.
It is not a lonesome place at all.
A Navajo house shabby and small?
It is Not!
Inside there's love,
Good laughter,
And *Big Talk.*
But best—
It's home
With an open door
And room for all.
A Castle could have no more.

I Am a Papago Girl

by Frances Kisto

I am a Papago girl.
I live in a Papago village.
I am thankful for it.
It may be a dry, desert village,
It may be lonesome.
The sadness may cover me
but I am thankful for it
because I am a Papago girl.

Walk Proud, Walk Straight, Let Your Thoughts Race

by Patty Harjo

Walk proud, walk straight, let your thoughts race
with the blue wind, but do not bare your soul to
your enemies.

The black mountain lion called night devours the
white rabbit of day. And the icy cold wind blows
over the still-warm, brown earth.

In restless dreams I called out his name.
Waking, I do not remember.

In my score of years
I have known not love
except wind, earth and darkness.

When I Was Young, My Father Said

by Bruce Ignacio

When I was young, my father said:
In the rivers, or much deeper than within these waters,
A people live, cursed within the spin
To get revenge, for they cannot live upon our land.
So, during the summer months, do not disturb
The Water People,
For they have an.odor that will make you feel blue and still.
Also, the Water Ones will take you in their arms
And put you to sleep within their land of motion.
When they do, they flee with joy.
They come from the water to laugh in triumph.

While they play, in the house I listen with my heart content.
They sound sad and, like their babies, left alone.
Father, why? Oh, why do they cry?
It's a trick they have used, time and time before,
But now the Water People will soon be gone
For their currents are slowly dying.
And now they have felt the vanishing of their land

For years and years,
But they will not be gone.
They will sleep beneath the ground,
And, at last, when all other peoples have left
This cruel land, they will rise up
And the Water People will start the world anew.

New Way, Old Way

by Dave Martin Nez

Beauty in the old way of life—
The dwellings they decorated so lovingly;
A drum, a clear voice singing,
And the sound of laughter.

You must want to learn from your mother,
You must listen to old men
   not quite capable of becoming white men.
The white man is not our father.
While we last, we must not die of hunger.
We were a very Indian, strong, competent
      people,
But the grass had almost stopped its growing,
The horses of our pride were near their end.

Indian cowboys and foremen handled Indian
      herds.
A cowboy's life appealed to them until
   economics and tradition clashed.
No one Indian was equipped to engineer the
   water's flow onto a man's allotment.
Another was helpless to unlock the gate.
The union between a hydro-electric plant and
Respect for the wisdom of the long-haired chiefs

Had to blend to build new enterprises
By Indian labor.

Those mighty animals graze once more
    upon the hillside.
At the Fair appear again our ancient costumes.
A full-blood broadcasts through a microphone
    planned tribal action.
Hope stirs in the tribe,
Drums beat and dancers, old and young
        step forward.

We shall learn all these devices the white man
        has,
We shall handle his tools for ourselves.
We shall master his machinery, his inventions,
    his skills, his medicine, his planning;
But we'll retain our beauty
And still be Indians!

Sorry About That

by Kenneth Kale

I've often wondered why it is said
that the Indian Spirit is broken and dead—
why such balderdash fills the air
when in their midst like a grizzly bear
is the sleeping red-skinned giant now on the
        prowl
an answer to a lone Kiowa's vengeful howl

And I wonder why BIA Zombies chose to pout
when it is evident we know all about

our red-skinned counterpart of Martin, Gregory,
   and Stokely rolled into one
Like an angry "Red Muslim" with work to be
   done

We see he has proven no fight is entirely in vain
if the cause is right and the guilty are blamed
where the grievance is brought before a federal
   judge
to where Bureaucrats move that would not otherwise budge

He taunts and laughs and spits in the face
of the land-hungry schemes of the white race
and shakes up their world with statements of fact
while chanting the redman's spirit is coming back

He has reawakened Indian interest in their land
new interest in their legal rights to the dirt and
   sand to
the need for extensive litigation and solid stand
lest he lose all to the encroaching white man

No chicken-feathered war bonnets hang in his
   den
this lone Indian who chills hearts black as sin
His fight has taken him there and back again
to be remembered with Crazy Horse, Geronimo
   and other great men

He is an Indian Legend in his own lifetime
a formidable foe and in his prime
I am happy to say he is a leader of mine
you will all know him by my rhyme

And with that—maybe I have said it all
except perhaps that he gets things done
and he doesn't quit a fight until it's won
He works without pay, does things his own way
and is considerate of some
He will readily call an ace an ace and a bum a
    bum—and like I say—gets considerable
    done
Federal land claims and legal suits everywhere
being filed—and upon his countenance is a heap
    big smile—

"Ha" says he "Sorry bout that."

Death

by Janie Bullis

Let it be, my father. You have left us alone on this world.
But go where you are headed for. Don't ever turn back to
    your children.
For there is only one trail that we can pass through.
Even though you've left us, we may follow you sometime.
And meet you in the place called Y'ah-k'ah, ya (paradise).

My Life

by Jeanne Baker

I was born
I will live
I will go
But who knows when.

War Signs

by Willie George

Last night my mother saw
War signs in the sky;
I was afraid to look up

But the moon was so yellow
And the stars so bright
I had to look.

Poem for Vietnam

by Ray Young Bear

i always miss the feeling
of friday on my mind.
the umbrella somewhere
in the dumps of south
vietnam. franco must be
here in a guy's heart.
the closest I got was
when i machine-gunned
the people waist deep
inside the brown swamp.
the castle where we drank
the sweet wine from giant
fish bowls. the old mansion
where his friend played
cards. the door closed from
his brothers and a knife
waking everything else
inside the throat so far

away. i have not held this
god that lies beside me.
only this rock that i heard
about stays and often i feel
as if it must be true.
the wrists are bleeding
and it rains for the tree.
his words are like my dreams
i can only sit there and
imagine so greatly. they were
ear close. i heard them talking
a couple of yards ahead of me.
my little brother and i hunted
while someone close was being
buried on the same hill where
we will end. it was a time when
strawberries came bearing no
actual meanings. a house with
words saying he trodded on
a land across the water.
i saw him the very day he
arrived. his boots still had
the mud of yesterday and i
stood still trying to
remember the things we used
to do. the fall came and one sunday he decided
to stick a rifle barrel in
his mouth and really silenced
our good-byes. the slender
bird within this people of
rainwater eyes prayed beside
the well. we spoke to each
other across our nearing
sleeps and april black

still walks inside memories.
i was out with the moon
when i scratched his back
knowing of sacrifices. the
children growing up drunk.

Loser

by David Reeves

In my own country I'm in a far off land
I'm strong but have no force or power
I win, yet remain a loser

At break of day I say goodnight
When I lie down I have a great fear of falling.

HE WHO MAKES A BEAST OF HIMSELF
GETS RID OF THE PAIN OF BEING A MAN.

MY WORDS ARE CHANGED
INTO DIRTY THOUGHTS

In the past, tribal children were forbidden to speak
their native languages in school. One government
boarding school punished students for this offense by
having them "scrub the boys' toilets with a tooth-
brush." The development of bilingual and bicultural
education, with texts and curriculum in Navajo, Lakota, Cherokee, and other tribal languages, is aimed at
halting this "cultural genocide." But, as these poignant
letters by two little Navajo girls testify, change has
been slow in coming. ("My Language: Is Navajo a

Dirty Word?," by Bertha Desiderio, *The Word Passer,*
Vol. I, No. 3, March–April, 1969, and "My Teacher Is
a Lizard," by Mary Lynn Blackburn, *Rough Rock
News,* Rough Rock, Az., Navajo Nation, Dec. 2, 1969.)

My Language: Is Navajo a Dirty Word?

by Bertha Desiderio

I came into this world as a Navajo child. As I grew up, I
learned to speak a language. This language I came to treas-
ure, to feel at ease when I spoke it, and it brought me an
identification as a true, proud Navajo. I spoke this language
before I heard another language called English. My parents
taught me how to pronounce the Navajo words right and
taught me what they meant. I treasured the language as I
went through my early youth, even though I was learning a
new language that I would need as I got through life, but
still, I never wanted to lose my own language.

When I conversed with this language that I treasured, I
was proud because it was mine and it was given to me by
my ancestors. I was never ashamed to speak my language,
because it was one with my pride and joy.

Today—I hate to say this—but I am ashamed to speak
Navajo in front of a group of Navajo students. The language
that I was proud of has been changed into a "twisted" language. These days it seems like I can't say anything in Navajo without getting embarrassed. When I do talk in Navajo,
my words are changed into dirty thoughts by people who do
not realize that our language is supposed to be a value for
us. Instead, they take our language as trash.

I wonder how students who twist their language into
dirty thoughts feel about their culture going down the drain.
Again I wonder if it ever bothers them not to take their cul-

ture into consideration. As an individual, I dread to see my culture fade out just because some of us students don't care to use our language as it is supposed to be used.

Are you really proud to be a Navajo? Then talk as if you took pride in your language.

My Teacher Is a Lizard

by Mary Lynn Blackburn

Mr. Gordon is a lizard. Mr. Gordon was a man at one time. Then he was so mean that he turned into a lizard. He went to school. Everybody laughed at him. He went to his house and looked in a mirror and laughed in lizard talk.

Chris is our teacher's aide and she is just a year old and she is funny. I think she is going to be a lizard too. With two lizards in the room, it is going to be funny. It is going to be hard to learn.

INDIAN EDUCATION

The late Senator Robert Kennedy described Indian education as "a national scandal." In *Our Brother's Keeper: The Indian in White America,* edited by Edgar S. Cahn (New York, Meridian-World, 1970), the results of this educational system are summed up by three factors: "The average educational level for all Indians under federal supervision is five school years. . . . Dropout rates are twice the national average. . . . The longer an Indian child stays in school, the further behind he gets." The day-to-day tragedy of school life is succinctly told in four newspaper items included here. ("Missing Children," *Talking Leaf*, Los Angeles Indian Center, March, 1969; "Youth Dies of Exposure" and "Three Kayenta Teachers Resign," *Navajo Times*, Jan. 29, 1970; "Why Must We Be Treated Like Monkeys?," *Sandpainter*, Navajo Nation, Sept. 5, 1969.)

Missing Children

The Riverside (California) Indian School has asked our assistance relative to four missing children. These children are students of the school.

These girls have been missing since "about Christmas time," and little information relative to their features has been received. The best data available at this time is that they all "look like Indians."

The names of the missing girls are:

> Lillian Norman
> Delores Dan
> Doycelyn Brewer (who has green eyes)
> Myra Jean George

The ages of these missing girls range from 15 to 16 and all are described as having "dark hair."

Youth Dies of Exposure

Kayenta, Arizona—Johnson Kee West, 11, a fourth-grade student at Kayenta Boarding School, was found dead on Tuesday morning, January 20, about 24 hours after he and four other boys had run away from the school. The boys were apparently trying to get to their homes on Black Mesa.

The boys left the school before breakfast on Monday

morning, January 19, but school officials did not find out they were missing until shortly after noon that day.

The acting principal had to attend a meeting that day and she delegated another woman to be acting principal. However, the person she delegated had to be in the classroom that morning. The teachers, in their daily attendance reports, reported the boys missing, but Mrs. Iva Marie Kingsley, who had been delegated acting principal, was not informed they were missing until she returned to the office shortly after noon.

Three of the boys—Louis (Boyd) Blackhat, Kee Tsosie Yazzie and James Lloyd Yazzie—were found in a hogan on Black Mesa about 3 A.M., the following morning.

The fourth boy—Nelford Smith—was found about 6 A.M. He appeared to be suffering from exposure and was taken to a hospital.

The dead boy was found about two hours later about 300–400 yards down from the top of the mesa. He was apparently trying to get back to Kayenta when he sat down to rest.

Three Kayenta Teachers Resign

Kayenta, Arizona—Three teachers at the Kayenta Elementary School who protested the school's ice cream policy have resigned, and the school continues the practice.

The policy which the three teachers protested was to give the children an ice cream cone when they went home on Friday night if they had had perfect attendance during the week.

The three teachers—Julia F. Marchant, Marie Letchko, and Janet M. Parsons—had charged that the ice cream policy was opposed to good educational practices, particularly on the Navajo reservation where children sometimes find it difficult to get to school each day.

But Jack Wilson, superintendent, defended the policy, saying that attendance had improved since the program was implemented, and that students were even showing up better scholastically as a result of the program.

"Why Must We Be Treated Like Monkeys?"

by Jr. Draper

Many articles are written concerning education for the Navajo boys and girls on the Navajo Reservation. I am a high school student attending Chinle High School. I like to go straight to school from my house, but the Chinle High School officials put up a big wire fence all around the school, where there is no gate between the Low Rent Housing and the Chinle High School. So lots of time some students are forced to climb over the fence which is eight feet high, with barbed wire running along the top. Many times my clothes were torn, and there were times when my hands and legs were cut by the sharp wire. I cannot understand why they would have a fence around our school, that is put on the reservation to help the Navajo children receive an education. If the school was really interested in my education, it seems to me that they would have put in a gate at least so that those of us who live in the Low Rent Housing Area would have a more sensible way of getting to school. (Why must we be treated like monkeys, when we are trying to get an education?)

Last year many of us received tribal clothing at tribal expense, but a lot of the clothing were torn to pieces on the public school fence. Why give us clothing if they are just going to get torn on the fence? We need a gate between the

Low Rent Housing Area and the Chinle High School campus. We hope that someone will at least give us the consideration and put in a gate so that I and my buddies can go to school without feeling fenced out.

THE SCHOOLS ARE FENCED IN: COMMUNITY CONTROL OF THE SCHOOLS

by Vance Randall

> "We often give lip service to this idea of 'self-determination,'" says Dr. Sophie Aberle, for thirty years an official and educational specialist for the Bureau of Indian Affairs. Community control of the schools by Indian tribes has become a national issue, but on the reservations it is still the exception, as the Apache educator Vance Randall, Chairman of the National Advisory Committee on BIA Kindergarten Program, indicates. ("The Schools Are Fenced In," by Vance Randall, a tribal leader of the "unrecognized" tribe of Verde Valley Apaches, in Central Az., unpublished and undated.)

What exactly does one [Indian] see in the BIA Kindergarten Program?

One of the first things that caught our senses was the specification that the Indian involvement in a decision-making and policy-making role was spelled out. This is the work that has united us. But we have come to find out that there are various interpretations of Indian involvement. Today, the promises of 1968 have not become a reality. But we are striving for the day when Indians will sit down and draw up a program and have a say in hiring with the BIA. Today it is still the game of "tokenism" and "symbolic participation," although there have been some slight changes in attitude, but these do not pacify the group.

The second thing that caught our senses is the bicultural and bilingual approach. A child needs self-pride and needs to know who he is. In earlier years, the practice of throwing away the blanket° was cultural genocide for our people. What kind of a solid, basic foundation can one have if he is degraded to the extent that what he has and is is not good?

And the hiring of Indian instructional aides, who in a sense are co-teachers, has been a tremendous morale boost to the people at the community level. They see one of their own kind in that school that has been an island by itself. Not to take anything away from the teachers and their degrees, the aide has become one of the most important persons in this program. He is the link to the community and the school so that a two-way communication can be set up where today we [Indians] know it is one-way. And the one-way today is of the lowest calibre. In the years this program has existed, tremendous changes have taken place as the aides have become leaders and truly a stimulus to the community.

The third thing that caught our senses ties in with the first two. And that is that the educational process is not only for the children but also for the parents and the community.

Schools I have seen are fenced in. There are two distinct and separate worlds. The parents need to cross that fence and become involved in their children's educational experiences. At the same time, there is the educational process of developing decision-making. When parents decide what day to go on a picnic—that will lead to the decisions of hir-

° In the nineteenth century tribesmen who fled the schools and reservations and returned to nature and the ancient ways were said by whites to "have gone back to the blanket." The forcing of children back to school was "throwing away the blanket."

ing and firing a principal or a curriculum change tomorrow. There will be a time, which will be soon, when we will have self-pride.

In this little program, we can see the Utopia we are looking for and striving for. We realize that there are a lot of criticisms about work through the OEO programs. Our thoughts as to this criticism has been that we [Indians] have a foot in the system where we have been ignored and as we discover and voice our rights then there is hope.

One day the Indians will be truly involved in the educational destiny of their children.

One day the Indians will truly run their own schools.

It is a time when Indians should make their own successes and mistakes. To that end we strive with integrity.

A NAVAJO MEDICINE MAN CURES HIS SON

In the nineteenth century, missionaries and educators sought to ban tribal religious beliefs and medicine ceremonies as "pagan rituals." Modern medicine has more recently recognized much of Indian medicine as biochemically and psychologically therapeutic. On the Navajo reservation, medicine men have worked with psychiatrists and healers with U.S. Public Health Service doctors to synthesize the ancient and modern healing arts. ("A Navajo Medicine Man Cures His Son," as told to Sidney M. Callaway, Gary Witherspoon and others, *Grandfather Stories*, Rough Rock, Az., Navajo Curriculum Center, 1970.)

"If my father were here, he could cure me," John told the Navajo nurse at the hospital as she bathed the sores on the little boy's body.

The doctors and the nurses were very good to John Kinsel. They knew that he was the son of a well-known medicine man, and they had placed John in a private room. Maybe he would not have been so lonely if he had been in a ward with other boys.

The physicians in the Navajo area, especially around Fort Defiance, co-operated with the medicine men as much as possible. They knew the medicine men had spent much of their lives preparing themselves for this noble work of curing their people of all kinds of sicknesses. The medicine men had been doing it before there were any hospitals or white physicians on the reservation. The doctors knew that the Navajo people respected the medicine men. Of course, there are some medicine men who are not good, just as there are doctors today who are not good.

Most of the Public Health Service physicians realized that the medicine men knew medical and health secrets which the white doctors never even heard of.

"John," said the nurse, "if it were not for these sores on your body, I'd say you were just plain homesick for your parents, your sheep dog, and to get out and herd sheep. I don't understand why these sores aren't getting better. They should be well by now. How long have you been in the hospital?"

"I came three days before the Easter holidays. I was going home. Remember?"

"Then you are homesick. I have noticed you sitting up in bed, just looking out the window. You *are* homesick."

"Miss Yellowhair, why can't my father come and take me home? He can make me well again in two or three days. I know he can," begged John.

Neither the nurse nor the doctor had time to make the trip to find John's father. But a pupil from near John's hogan was home for Easter, and he told John's big brother about John being in the hospital.

John's parents came to the doctor's office that very day, explaining why they should take the boy home for a Navajo ceremony. They told the doctor that they had the medicine that would heal their son.

It was true that John was no better after two weeks of care at the hospital. The sores were still there. The fever was even worse. The doctor had changed treatments several times. But he never had had a patient with sores so hard to cure. The boy really was sick. Maybe the medicine man *did* have the medicine.

The doctor gave the medicine man a brief history of the case. He made some suggestions, which may not have been heeded. Then he gave John a temporary release from the hospital. John was to return for a checkup before going back to school.

Most Navajo ceremonials last from two to nine days. John's father was a medicine man and he was to treat his son in a ceremony which would last only two days.

Soon after his return home, John was feeling better. First, he was well cared for and loved. His relatives were around him, and they told him he soon would be well again. The relatives planned every detail of the ceremony.

True, he had only his sheepskin for a bed, whereas, at the hospital, his bed had had spotless white sheets. Everything there had to be germ-proof. The very air he breathed smelled like medicine. The food must have been good for him, but it tasted different even from the food he had learned to eat at school. Just when he was beginning to like the food at school, he was sent to the hospital where the food was different.

John had been taught that each ceremonial chant had

come directly from the Holy People. To be in harmony with the Holy People he must be free from all ills and evils.

John had seen the ceremony succeed for others, and he knew it would work for him. With his father doing the ceremony, he knew he would get well. He knew this because the Holy People had done it that way from the beginning. It seemed that he had put on the moccasins of the Holy People, had walked with them along the pollen path, and had breathed the strength of the sun.

The doctors and the nurses at the hospital had been good to him. They had done everything to make him comfortable. He was happy there, in a way. But, with his people, he found true happiness and a feeling of belonging.

His father knew the right herbs to use and how to prepare the medicine for the sores. After a few days, John was well and happy again.

The medicine man took his son back to the hospital office as he had promised. The physician was surprised but happy to see the boy completely well again.

The doctor thought, "The medicine men have something that we doctors do not have. I wish I knew. Possibly, someday, working together, we will know, too."

▲▲▲▲▲▲▲▲▲▲▲▲▲▲▲▲▲▲▲▲

V. THE LAWS
OF LIFE:
TRIBAL
AND LEGAL

LIVE AS YOUR WISE FOREFATHERS
LIVED BEFORE YOU

by Pontiac

"Life is sacred," said Miss Indian America for 1967, a
Taos Pueblo college girl, Wahleah Lujan; "Let us be
walking images of our beautiful way of life. Hold fast
to your lands, to your sacred ways." In her religiosity,
she was echoing the vision of Pontiac, who delineated
the inseparable bonds between belief and life that still
guide modern Indian movements. (*The Conspiracy of
Pontiac*, by Francis Parkman, unpublished and undated, pp. 204–7.)

The Indian conceived an eager desire to learn wisdom from
the Master of Life; but, being ignorant where to find him,
he had recourse to fasting, dreaming, and magical incanta-
tions. By these means it was revealed to him, that, by moving forward in a straight, undeviating course, he would
reach the abode of the Great Spirit. He told his purpose to
no one, and, having provided the equipment of a hunter—
gun, powder-horn, ammunition, and a kettle for preparing
his food—he set out on his errand.

For some time, he journeyed on in high hope and confidence. On the evening of the eighth day, he stopped by
the side of a brook at the edge of a meadow, where he
began to make ready his evening meal, when, looking up, he
saw three large openings in the woods before him, and three

well-beaten paths which entered them. He was much surprised; but his wonder increased, when, after it had grown dark, the three paths were more clearly visible than ever. Remembering the important object of his journey, he could neither rest nor sleep; and, leaving his fire, he crossed the meadow, and entered the largest of the three openings.

He had advanced but a short distance into the forest, when a bright flame sprang out of the ground before him and arrested his steps. In great amazement, he turned back, and entered the second path, where the same wonderful phenomenon again encountered him; and now, in terror and bewilderment, yet still resolved to persevere, he took the last of the three paths.

On this he journeyed a whole day without interruption, when at length, emerging from the forest, he saw before him a vast mountain of dazzling whiteness. So precipitous was the ascent, that the Indian thought it hopeless to go farther, and looked around him in despair.

At that moment, he saw, seated at some distance above, the figure of a beautiful woman arrayed in white, who arose as he looked upon her, and thus accosted him: "How can you hope, encumbered as you are, to succeed in your design? Go down to the foot of the mountain, throw away your gun, your ammunition, your provisions, and your clothing; wash yourself in the stream which flows there, and you will then be prepared to stand before the Master of Life."

The Indian obeyed and again began to ascend among the rocks, while the woman, seeing him still discouraged, laughed at his faintness of heart, and told him that, if he wished for success, he must climb by the aid of one hand and one foot only. After great toil and suffering, he at length found himself at the summit. The woman had disappeared, and he was left alone.

A rich and beautiful plain lay before him, and at a little

distance he saw three great villages, far superior to the squalid wigwams of the Delawares. As he approached the largest, and stood hesitating whether he should enter, a man gorgeously attired stepped forth, and, taking him by the hand, welcomed him to the celestial abode. He then conducted him into the presence of the Great Spirit, where the Indian stood confounded at the unspeakable splendor which surrounded him. The Great Spirit bade him be seated, and thus addressed him:

"I am the Maker of heaven and earth, the trees, lakes, rivers, and all things else. I am the Maker of mankind; and because I love you, you must do my will. The land on which you live I have made for you, and not for others. Why do you suffer the white men to dwell among you? My children, you have forgotten the customs and traditions of your forefathers. Why do you not clothe yourselves in skins, as they did, and use the bows and arrows, and the stone-pointed lances, which they used? You have bought guns, knives, kettles, and blankets from the white men, until you can no longer do without them; and, what is worse, you have drunk the poison fire-water, which turns you into fools. Fling all these things away; live as your wise forefathers lived before you. . . ."

THE WHITE MAN'S WAY:
"WE GAVE THEM MEAT, THEY GAVE US POISON"

by Sago-yo-watha (Red Jacket)

Sago-yo-watha (Red Jacket) was a "law giver" of the Iroquois, whose name meant "He Who Keeps Us Alert." A Seneca orator, he spoke "With a voice as low, as gentle and caressing, as e'er won a maiden's lips," wrote an envious contemporary. His speech to the Moravian Church missionary, Reverend Cram, in the early 1800's, pointed to the conflict between Christian deed and Indian belief. (*The Indian and the White Man*, edited by Wilcomb E. Washburn, New York, Doubleday and Company, 1964, pp. 211–13.)

Friend and Brother: It was the will of the Great Spirit that we should meet together this day. He orders all things and has given us a fine day for our council. He has taken his garment from before the sun and caused it to shine with brightness upon us. Our eyes are opened, that we see clearly; our ears are unstopped, that we have been able to hear distinctly the words you have spoken. For all these favors we thank the Great Spirit; and Him *only*.

Brother: This council fire was kindled by you. It was at your request that we came together at this time. We have listened with attention to what you have said. You requested us to speak our minds freely. This gives us great joy, for we now consider that we stand upright before you and can speak what we think. All have heard your voice, and all speak to you now as one man. Our minds are agreed. . . .

There was a time when our forefathers owned this great island. Their seats extended from the rising to the setting sun. The Great Spirit had made it for the use of Indians. He had created the buffalo, the deer, and other animals for food. He had made the bear and the beaver. Their skins served us for clothing. He had scattered them over the country and taught us how to take them. He had caused the earth to produce corn for bread. All this He had done for his red children, because He loved them. If we had some disputes about our hunting ground, they were generally settled without the shedding of much blood. But an evil day came upon us. Your forefathers crossed the great water and landed on this island. Their numbers were small. They found friends and no enemies. They told us they had fled from their own country for fear of wicked men and had come here to enjoy their religion. They asked for a small seat. We took pity on them, granted their request; and they sat down amongst us. We gave them corn and meat, they gave us poison in return.

The white people had now found our country. Tidings were carried back and more came amongst us. Yet, we did not fear them. We took them to be friends. They called us brothers. We believed them and gave them a larger seat. At length, their numbers had greatly increased. They wanted more land; they wanted our country. Our eyes were opened and our minds became uneasy. Wars took place. Indians were hired to fight against Indians and many of our people were destroyed. They also brought strong liquor amongst us. It was strong and powerful and has slain thousands.

Brother: Our seats were once large and yours were small. You have now become a great people and we have scarcely a place left to spread our blankets. You have got our country, but are not satisfied; you want to force your religion upon us.

Brother: Continue to listen.

You say that you are sent to instruct us how to worship the Great Spirit agreeably to His mind, and, if we do not take hold of the religion which you white people teach, we shall be unhappy hereafter. You say that you are right and we are lost. How do we know this to be true? We understand that your religion is written in a book. If it was intended for us as well as you, why has not the Great Spirit given to us, and not only to us, but why did He not give to our forefathers, the knowledge of that book, with the means of understanding it rightly? We only know what you tell us about it. How shall we know when to believe, being so often deceived by the white people?

Brother: You say there is but one way to worship and serve the Great Spirit. If there is but one religion, why do you white people differ so much about it? Why are not all agreed, as you can all read the book?

Brother: We do not understand these things.

We are told that your religion was given to your forefathers, and has been handed down from father to son. We also have a religion, which was given to our forefathers, and has been handed down to us their children. We worship in that way. It teaches us to be thankful for all the favors we receive, to love each other, and to be united. We never quarrel about religion.

Brother: The Great Spirit has made us all, but He has made a great difference between His white and red children. He has given us different complexions and different customs. To you He has given the arts. To these He has not opened our eyes. We know these things to be true. Since He has made so great a difference between us in other things, why may we not conclude that He has given us a different religion according to our understanding? The Great Spirit does right. He knows what is best for His children; we are satisfied.

Brother: We do not wish to destroy your religion, or take it from you. We only want to enjoy our own.

Brother: We are told that you have been preaching to the white people in this place. These people are our neighbors. We are acquainted with them. We will wait a little while and see what effect your preaching has upon them. If we find it does them good, makes them honest and less disposed to cheat Indians, we will then consider again of what you have said.

Brother: You have now heard our answer to your talk and this is all we have to say at present.

As we are going to part, we will come and take you by the

hand, and hope the Great Spirit will protect you on your journey and return you safe to your friends.

THE MISSIONARY IN A CULTURAL TRAP

by Vine Deloria, Jr.

"God Is Red" was a slogan popularized by Vine Deloria, Jr., the third generation of his family to study for
the ministry. His grandfather was one of the first Lakota Christian ministers on the prairies. His father, Reverend Vine Deloria, Sr., is an archdeacon of the Epis-
copal Church, who has said: "Sometimes I despair of
the white man's ever becoming a Christian." Like his
father, Vine Deloria, Jr., believes that "Religion is an
intellectual abstraction to the white man. It is not spiritual to him." This critique was written in reply to an
article "The Indian in a Cultural Trap," in a church
magazine; but the magazine refused to print it. (*The
Missionary in a Cultural Trap*, by Vine Deloria, Jr.,
printed privately, undated.)

Missionaries have been chosen—and wisely so—as targets in
the War on Ignorance conducted by the Indian people of
this country. The good of the country as a whole demands
such action, since these people can be the breeding ground
for doctrines of intolerance, arrogance, and unwise policies
regarding the American Indian. But, if anyone thinks that
all that is needed is education, he has a few surprises coming. The missionary has attitudes of his own, and any attempt to help understand cultural differences had better be
preceded by a careful study of the cultural and theological
confusion in church mission programs. It is these factors, far
more than lack of education, that have made mission at-

tempts quite depressing and they are still creating frustrations and confusion.

The missionary and his ideas are attractive from a distance. Examined more carefully, however, that missionary and those ideas are something less than perfect. Missionaries have a tradition, for example, of wanting Indian people to want the same things they want. Those of us accustomed to the Indian culture, where the right to be different is taken for granted, are tempted to look upon conformity to the missionaries' ideas as a pleasant means of getting along in modern society. In a culture proud of the tradition of remaining silent unless one is asked by one's peers for one's opinion, the ability of the missionary to be an instant expert on all subjects with us, experience can look like a noble tradition. Moreover, in the midst of a calm and contemplative life, the ability to spend a lifetime in monotonous repetition of the same basic work can be taken to represent a form of high wisdom and security. It is comforting, but, alas, not correct, to think that wisdom can be had simply by obeying theological doctrines and disciplines.

The Indian culture respects the honest man. We speak with pride of the fact that we have not broken a single treaty, that we have kept our word, while the United States Government has broken over four hundred treaties. Missionary culture, as I have seen it, does not respect the truth. In an acquisitive society, the doctrine is "every man for himself and the devil take the hindmost." So the truth is always submerged in favor of the urge to escape the devil. . . .

Needless to say, the missionaries are above performing any of the routine tasks of the community. They have a dangerous task that only they can perform. As Sören Kierkegaard would have said, or maybe did say, "They must by their doctrines and preaching fool both God and man." If this isn't dangerous, we are at a loss to explain. When they are talking about things they don't know about, they are kings of the hill. In twentieth-century Indian culture, the missionary is an anachronism, yet the ideals and attitudes of the missionary persist in what remains of the mission program of the churches. The man who is ready to remain silent on subjects he doesn't know anything about is not fulfilling the missionary image of what a missionary should be. . . .

The experience of a Catholic priest on the Wind River reservation who wrote an article for *America* magazine illustrates how expounding on a subject one is unfamiliar with can work. After having been on the Wind River reservation for a whole four years, he is an "expert" on a culture that has maintained itself for thousands of years. The basic complaint of this priest is that the Indian culture is one of sharing. . . . Red Cloud, in one of his more profound statements said, "You must begin anew and put away the wisdom of your fathers. You must lay up food and forget the hungry; when your house is built, your storerooms filled, then look around for a neighbor whom you can take advantage of, and seize all he has." [See *The Long Death*, by Ralph Andrist, New York, Macmillan, 1964.]

In the American society, missionaries are paid by what is called "Sunday Collections" based chiefly on what church members give during the church services. It is distributed to missionaries by giving them what is left over after the administrative expenses have been paid. The collections are tax-free. . . . Each church mission station owns a plot of ground which is also tax-free. Last year, churches raised a considerable amount of money for mission activities, so that they were able to pay their missionaries about half of a living wage. . . .

There are about a million missionaries on each reservation, a good deal of them Catholic. Farmington, New Mexico, has, at last count, twenty-six different churches, all trying to convince the handful of Navajos that they alone have the true doctrine.

The various tribes are thinking of publishing a booklet discussing the problems in the mission field. One of the chief problems, certainly, is the number of missionaries employed in the mission field. The booklet will blame the number of diverse doctrines in or similar to the Christian religion for the busybody activities of the missionaries. It will add, however, that qualified missionaries often miss the unlimited opportunities to understand the Indian culture because they lack the humility to listen and insist on talking all the time. . . .

The missionaries' problems in understanding other cultures is notorious. In the early days in Europe, the Franks were given a choice between death and Christian baptism. During the Crusades, the Arabian culture was regarded as being in league with the devil, and it is well-known that the library at Alexandria was burned by zealous missionaries since it contained elements of a culture they did not wish to understand. . . .

We who have inherited Indian culture have often been tempted to remake others after our own image. Since we are trying very hard not to make such a mistake with the missionary, we have been led to conclude that any attempt to get the missionary to adapt to Indian culture would be a repetition of that mistake. If avoiding the mistakes of the past were enough to guarantee that one can avoid the mistakes of the present, the problem would be simpler; but, unfortunately, things do not always work out that way.

Some adaptation is a necessity for the missionary. The right to call private property everyone's is not the red man's prerogative; it is a universal mandate originally advocated by Jesus of Nazareth. A man must be able to take pride in his generosity and feel he is a contributing member of his society. But no one, not even a missionary, can be a profitable member of society so long as he insists that it is his privilege to keep all his possessions for himself and not share them with those who are less fortunate. We do not expect miracles— we would be willing to settle for fifty percent at present. Say if a man has two coats and his neighbor asks for one, and he only gives one, we would be satisfied.

The missionaries' problems are not a matter of inherited characteristics. Missionaries are very much like anyone else. They are not "selfish and greedy" of Indian imagination. They have no great wisdom that they receive by being ordained. If they are to succeed, they have to be untrained and they have to learn to relax as much as anyone else. One Indian has said that eighty percent of those who are willing to learn and listen while on Indian reservations are successful in learning something about Indian culture.

There are some missionaries in the church who would be acceptable on any reservation. There are others who are above average. Yet the overall picture of the churches is not a pretty one. For many clergy, the theological doctrines are a trap that keep them from being human.

RELIGION OF THE PEOPLE

by Herbert Blatchford

Not too many generations ago, a Holy Man said, "You ask me to plough the earth. Shall I take a knife and tear my mother's breast? Then, when I die, she will not take me to her bosom, to rest." It is this affinity of Mother Earth and the religion of the people (the

Dineh, as the Navajo call themselves) that is celebrated by Herbert Blatchford, a descendant of Navajo
headmen and a founder of the National Indian Youth
Council. Blatchford is director of the Gallup (New
Mexico) Indian Community Center. ("Religion of the
People," by Herbert Blatchford, unpublished and undated.)

My opinion on Indian religion is based only upon my experience with the Navajo people. The thoughts and beliefs of a
number of tribes in America may be abstracted out of the
Navajo beliefs only in a general way, for the specific beliefs
and rituals belong to the different tribes alone.

Indian religions are based primarily on the premise of fertility. Because the keynote is fertility, we must therefore
think in terms of all elements, tangible and intangible,
which lend a part in the fertility of all living matter. In light
of this reasoning, we have in Indian religions male and female rains, male and female winds, as well as male and female species of animals. As many peoples of the world think
of nature in terms of "Mother Earth," so do these people.
Since nearly all things are thought of in terms of life and fertility, the Indian peoples tend to value the intangibles of nature to the highest degree of human attainment. This makes
them a spiritually oriented people. The best of thoughts,
ideas, and behavior tend to be of a moral nature not necessarily conforming to the material logic in pattern of behavior.

The basis of the complex nature of ritual and ceremony
stems from constant observance of nature and its behavior
over a long period of time, and not so much from idealizing
the behavior of nature. It is generally understood among the
Indians that we do not know the "why's" of nature, but we
can observe and live by the "how's" of nature. The abstract
forms and symbols used in ceremony and ritual are derived

from the natural forms found in nature. The same may be said for the actions and physical manipulation involved in the dances, although much of the actions are modified to fit human abilities.

It is difficult to assume that the sounds in the songs used in Indian dancing and ceremony have also been taken from the sounds of nature. I prefer to think of them in terms of sounds developed by humans to impress some significant material upon the human mind. The patterns of Indian music are made up of tones which are pleasant and soothing to the Indian senses, and which tends, in an indigenous way, to bring out the aesthetic qualities in vocal manipulations. The crescendos and diminuendos in Indian music resemble the animal and whistling wind vibrations in nature. Variation in pitch covers tones which start at a bass guttural sound, and in some instances the pitch is on a high falsetto note. Intervals used in Indian songs may vary from the octave to quarter-tones, and, in some of the music, the interval might be in eighth-tones, but for this writer this is very difficult to detect. Though this may sound rather absurd, for it would appear to some people that Indian music is bordering on noise or discord, it would be well to recognize here that the set of English vowels found in the Navajo language takes on four different levels of phonetic values; thus we have a greater variation in the intervals of Indian music than in Anglo music.

To say that certain animals and symbols are thought of as sacred seems to me a bit superficial, for, in a large sense, the whole universe is sacred; thus, all things in the universe are sacred. All animals have a place in Indian lore, but only when they are connected with certain ceremonies are they sacred in terms of individual circumstances. To the mountain people, the bear is a symbol of strength and courage; to the plains people, the coyote is a symbol of slyness and trickery; but these characteristics may also be traits of humans—hence the personification of animals in our spiritual stories. Animals are a living core of Indian religions.

In view of the above dissertation, one may think that the Indian shows some discretion before slaying an animal. This is true to a large degree. The Indian has tried and is still trying to live in harmony with the universe, and, in the past, in times of natural abundance, the Indian did slay animals only to satisfy their needs of ritual, food, shelter, and clothing. Since confinement to specific land areas, the natural turnover of supply and demand has become a thing of the past, but thoughts of pursuing harmony are still in the minds of the people. This has been well-defined in the past: When the land is sick, the people are sick, and when the people are sick, the land is sick; it is up to the people to beseech the Universal Guardian to restore harmony and well-being.

Because of his belief in harmony and in following the natural course of events, the Indian does not project his aims and aspirations far into the distant future, but rather he thinks in terms of the present and the past so as not to disrupt the blessedness of harmony. Time is more a proving factor than a controlling factor to the Indian way of living.

The so-called myths and legends of the Indian people are made up of behavior references to humans as well as to animals. These stories also pursue in some detail what may be thought of as mysticism or magic. To fully understand these stories, which to my mind are designed to teach moral behavior, a person has to think in terms of Universal Life Continuity, that is, that there is a related continuity of life and well-being between all living matter, and that this life and well-being are dependent upon all organic and inorganic matter. We may see, then, that the universe is thought of as a whole made up of composite parts, and the relationship of the parts are focused into the whole by the use of spiritual stories which utilize ideas about all living species along with inorganic material. The natural balance between the parts of the whole, which is maintained by nature, is recognized throughout the stories, and the recognition of this balance tends to lead the listener to observe moral behavior. These stories are not told with these specific aims in mind, but they are told with a general pattern in view which leaves opportunity for the individual to organize innately his pattern of perception.

OATH OF OFFICE OF THE PUEBLOS

translated by Joe Sando

Laws, to the tribal Indian, were and are exacting and humane. In the Pueblo Oath of Office, translated by the Jemez Pueblo historian and writer Joe Sando, the elected official had no power but his wisdom and "the fist of your hand," for before the white man came, with his laws, there were no prisons. And the official pledges to "cherish and protect all that contains life, from the lowliest crawling creatures to the human." ("The Pueblo People," by Joe Sando, *The Indian Historian*, Vol. II, No. 3, Fall, 1969. By permission of author.)

Into your care we entrust our land and our people. Regardless of whether you are poor, or lack the oratory to express yourself fluently, you will to the best of your ability be the protector, impartially, for your people. The stranger who comes into our land will become as one of your people, regardless of race, color or creed, and you will give unto them the same protection and rights as you would your own. You will cherish and protect all that contains life, from the lowliest crawling creatures to the human. By hasty word or deed you will refrain from hurting the feelings, both mentally and physically, of your people. In times when you, to the best of your ability and judgment, have resorted to every means to correct an individual who through stubborness remains contrary to the point of disrespect for the office you hold and would through his action be a bad example to his fellow man, you will question him four times whether he will continue to set aside peaceful, intelligent reasoning. If his answer is "yes," the four times, then you may strike him with the fist of your hand, and four times, if necessary.

THE LAWS OF THE INDIANS

by Wamblee Wicasa "Eagle Man" Ed McGaa

> Some of the tribes have attempted to codify their tribal laws in modern legal terminology. It has been difficult, for these tribal laws were based on human needs and religious imperatives, not political abstractions and property rights. Wamblee Wicasa (Ed McGaa), a Lakota lawyer and religionist, describes the conflicts and incongruities between tribal and white legal systems and beliefs. ("Suddenly Subject to New Laws," by Ed McGaa, *Great Plains Observer*, Jan., 1969, pp. 12–13.)

American Indians have a legal relationship with the United States Government unlike any other group of citizens in the nation. To discuss jurisdiction—tribal jurisdiction, state jurisdiction, and federal jurisdiction—Indian affairs and jurisdiction must be considered in their historical perspective. As acculturation and assimilation into the dominant non-Indian civilization progressed, the question of jurisdiction—

state, federal, or tribal—varied in depth and effectiveness.

In colonial times, the eastern Indian signed treaty agreements with the colonial governments. Traditionally, the Indian residing in the original thirteen states has looked to state and local government for services and legal jurisdiction.

After the thirteen colonies multiplied and expanded westward, the federal government made treaties with the Indian nations. Many of these treaties established large federal Indian reservations and the provision of certain services in exchange for large areas of land. Many treaties "granted" large areas of land to the tribes in exchange for cessation of the American Indian's determined and magnificent effort to protect his natural rights.

Before attempting to discuss jurisdiction, law within the Indian tribe itself must be considered before the advent of the *wasichu* (white man).

Every Indian nation had its own particular customs, but the legal functions of the Sioux will be given as quite representative of the plains Indian tribes. The plains people had a common religion and, since this was at the basis of the tribal code, customs pertaining to rights and legal duties do not differ to a large extent from tribe to tribe among the Sioux, Crow, Cheyenne, Blackfoot, and related tribes.

Indians lived by the axiom that no single person should endanger the people. No individual should lure an enemy to camp or drive away game. Crime was rare. Most property was communally owned and theft was almost unheard of. Stealing horses from the enemy was honorable and was often the task assigned to a young warrior aspiring to the mark of manhood, but stealing from one's own people was almost unthinkable. Murder usually was caused by jealousy and was punished by banishment. Banishment amounted to a death sentence, since an individual cast adrift on the cold, harsh prairie was fair game for trophy-seeking enemies. The aggrieved family decided the fate of the murderer in many cases.

Unpardonable sins were allowing anyone to go hungry, disrespect for the aged, abandoning children of dead parents, and returning alone from war after one's comrades have been slain. Irreverence toward the Great Spirit (*Wakan Tanka*) or religious articles was beyond the thoughts of any warrior well-accustomed to a natural religion wherein his leaders, medicine men, and chiefs commonly forecast events and performed acts that would promptly be classified as "miracles" in this day and age. Generosity, bravery, moral integrity, and fortitude were the tribe's four cardinal virtues and were well-practiced.

The Sioux had an elaborate system of warrior societies that picked their members according to deeds and devotion to the tribe. The older, experienced societies had a major influence upon tribal law. The Silent Eaters of the Hunkpapa were a dinner group which discussed the welfare of the tribe and made recommendations. Sitting Bull was a member of this society. Every year, camp police were appointed whose duty was to insure order in camp movement and lodge placement. They punished petty law-breakers and offenders. Any major crime was dealt with by the chief, who was advised by an older society composed of the village elders. In communal living, there were few secrets and usually the truth was brought forth from both sides.

From this simple, yet complex dignity, the oldest minority group in America suddenly became subject to new laws from a vastly different culture.

As early as 1832, the Supreme Court ruled that the Indian tribes were recognized and considered as "distinct, independent, political communities" and went on to state "that the Constitution, by declaring treaties already made as well as those to be made to be the supreme law of the land, has adopted and sanctioned the previous treaties with the Indian nations and consequently admits their rank among those powers who are capable of making treaties." "Treaty" and "nation" were applied in the same sense to Indians as to foreign nations.

Indian tribes were regarded as separate and sovereign nations. Each Indian nation's treaty with the United States must be judged on its own merits.

"LAW OF THE OUTLAWS" OF THE CHEROKEES

by Jack F. and Anna G. Kilpatrick

> One of every two American Indians is arrested every year. The national "arrest rate" per 100,000 population of whites is 2,739 and for Indians is 51,090 (*Uniform Crime Report*, FBI, 1960). Although the vast majority of arrests are for petty charges (vagrancy, drunkenness, disorderly conduct, etc.), these statistics help explain the origin of the "Law of the Outlaws" of the Cherokees. (*Run Toward The Nightland: Magic of the Oklahoma Cherokees*, by Jack F. and Anna G. Kilpatrick, Dallas, Tex., Southern Methodist University Press, 1967, pp. 108–10.)

Outlawry in the Cherokee hills has found its historians, literary and oral. Most have thoroughly misunderstood what they reported. The Cherokees have no weakness for homicide: Their chief failing is a touchiness in a fantastic degree on the question of their rights. The lawlessness that marred the pages of Cherokee history for a century after The Removal is not a testimony to any innate love of bloodshed in Cherokees, but rather to their astonishing ability to prolong a subterranean civil war that had its root in the question of whether or not to collaborate with the white man.

The white man who forced them from their homes in the Southeast set the stage for intramural bloodshed in the West. But he very obligingly did more than that: He stoked the fire that he had kindled. The jagged and roadless hills of the Cherokee Nation provided refuge for the wanted (and the unwanted) from the United States who added their guns to those of the Indian factions or went into business for themselves. Even as late as the days of the Great Depression, bank robbers and metropolitan gangsters made frequent use of the caves and coves of the Cherokee hills.

In the old Cherokee Nation, each district had law enforcement machinery guided by an elected official called a *di:da:ni:yi:sgi* ("one who apprehends them"). His life was an adventurous one, and sometimes short. Many of the notorious scofflaws were master conjurers as well as excellent marksmen. It paid any peace officer dealing with the likes of these to be as knowing in his magic as in his shooting.

Some manhunters were probably medicine men themselves, and knew how to get the conjuring drop on their quarries. If they were not, they could go to some good law-loving sorcerer who would "remake" tobacco for them to moisten and rub upon their bodies or to smoke toward the concealed outlaws.

Now! Screech Owl! Here! Here! Here! Here!
You are a great Wizard!
Always in the middle of the night You pass by.
Now! Brown Screech Owl! Very quickly You have
just come to put the White Ancient Tobacco
in my pipe.
Now! Brown Screech Owl! (Ha! He overcame it!)
You are a great Wizard!

Now You and I have just come to lift up the
   White Smoke.
You and I have just come to extract the souls
   of the Seven Those-Who-Take!

Undoubtedly there exist a sizable number of charms for
assisting persons accused of crime in their efforts to avoid
capture, but seldom is one of these to be found written
down. An example, carefully penciled in a well-preserved
stationery tablet that came from the vicinity of Sugar Mountain at the northern end of Tenkiller Lake is especially in-
teresting, for its label reads: "This is to use to make officers
of the law forget and to hide from them (merely to be said),
and also to help in a wrong against the people if they fight
back."

Nearly the whole of the Cherokee attitude toward law is
expressed or implied here: One violates a law in the legitimate expression of, or in the defense of, one's natural rights;
therefore, the law is at fault, not its violator. Since it is the
law that commits a "wrong against the people," its violator
is entitled to all the assistance he can get, supernatural or
otherwise. One is easily persuaded that if a medieval sei-
gneur had had Cherokee serfs, he would have had to contend with a Jacquerie every day of his life—for however
long that would have been.

The text of the Sugar Mountain charm is simply this:

Black Yellow Mockingbird!
Your lonely souls are confused!

THE ORIGIN AND DEVELOPMENT
OF THE NAVAJO TRIBAL GOVERNMENT

> Once upon a time, tribal government was based on the
> concept, "Treat all people as though they were related
> to you" (Navajo saying). The modern "Tribal Coun-
> cils" were established not by the tribes, but by the
> U.S. Government in order to sign treaties, oil leases,
> and the like, as this document issued by the Navajo
> tribe, in the early 1960's, notes. (*The Origin and Devel-
> opment of the Navajo Tribal Government,* Navajo
> tribe, Window Rock, Az., undated.)

A little over a century ago, the territory occupied by the Navajo people became a part of the United States. At that
time, and previously, the Navajo Tribe did not exist in the
ordinary political sense. There was a group of people sharing a common language and culture, but political organization apparently did not extend beyond local bands led by
headmen called *naat'aanii.* The headmen enjoyed varying
amounts of power based on their persuasive ability, but no
powers of coercion were attached to the office, the position
of headman was not hereditary, and coalitions of headmen
were probably few and of short duration. In short, the Tribe
did not constitute a political entity.

According to legend, the Tribe was once more closely
knit politically under the *naachid,* an organization report-
edly composed of twelve Peace Chiefs and twelve War
Chiefs, *elected* for life. It is said that the *naachid* gathered
periodically for ceremonials and council, and that such con-
ventions were dominated by one or another category of
naat'aanii, as circumstances might require. If such an organization was indeed functional in recent times it quite appar-

ently was not a potent force in Navajo affairs at the time the United States Government first entered the picture in 1846.

In fact, lack of formal political organization, and especially of responsible tribal leadership, constituted a serious problem for American military and administrative personnel charged with responsibility for treaty-making, control, and program direction. An agreement with one headman or band, or even with a group of headmen or bands, was not binding upon other Navajos who had not themselves been parties to the same agreement. . . .

The need for creation of a representative governing body had existed for many years, but the concept did not fit within the context of traditional Navajo social organization, and it was not until 1921 that a motive presented itself sufficiently compelling to overcome the inertia that had previously prevented steps toward the institution of tribal government.

In 1921, oil was discovered within the boundaries of the original Treaty Reservation, and the Midwest Refining Company was authorized to negotiate with the Indians of the San Juan (Northern Navajo) jurisdiction for an oil and gas development lease. A "general council" (i.e., assembly) of the Indians resident in that jurisdiction was called and a lease was approved for oil and gas purposes on 4,800 acres of land.

The calling of the "general council" no doubt met the requirement set forth in Article X of the Treaty of 1868 which provided that "no future treaty for the cession of any portion or part of the Reservation herein described, which may be held in common, shall be of any validity or force against said Indians unless agreed to and executed by at least three-fourths of all the adult male Indians occupying or interested in the same. . . ." However, the use of a "general council" as a medium for securing the approval of the Tribe to leases and other actions affecting tribal resources was clumsy and actually limited in its application on a reservation-wide basis. . . .

During 1922, a "business council" composed of Chee Dodge, Charlie Mitchell, and Dugal Chee Bekiss acted on behalf of the Tribe in the negotiation of [oil] leases.

However, the legality of the "business council" was questionable, and on January 27, 1923, Commissioner of Indian Affairs Charles H. Burke promulgated a document entitled "Regulations Relating to the Navajo Tribe of Indians." It was approved on the same date by Assistant Secretary of the Interior, F. M. Goodwin.

However, a few months later, a new set of regulations was issued over the signature of Acting Commissioner E. B. Merritt, and these were approved on April 24, 1923, by Secretary of the Interior Hubert Work.

The first meeting of this group [the Business Council—eds.] took place on July 7, 1923, at which time it adopted a resolution authorizing the Commissioner to the Navajo Tribe (a position established in conformity with the council regulations of 1923) to sign oil and gas leases on behalf of the Tribe. The Secretary of the Interior was authorized and requested by the same resolution to advertise a number of tracts for lease purposes. Of these, two tracts produced oil, and for many years the first tract authorized by the tribal council in 1923 remained the only producing oil wells on the Navajo Reservation, and these provided a large part of the tribal funds which accumulated in the Treasury between 1921 and 1957.

"THE REAL ISSUES OF THE CAMPAIGN"

Tribal elections may imitate all the hoopla and rhetoric of white political campaigns today. But, much of the politicking has been modified through acculturation, or "Indianized." Religious beliefs and tribal clan ties, unstated but implicit, often decide the campaigns, so that in the same elections conservative Republicans and liberal Democrats may be voted into office. The tone of elections is captured in a tribal campaign poster for Webster Two Hawk, chairman, Rosebud Sioux of South Dakota.

Invitation to you
for All-Indian Rally
At St. Francis Gym
Tuesday Night, Oct. 21
at 7:30 P.M.

All the Buffalo and Beef you can eat

Very Special Announcement
for all Reservation People:

Come and Hear Webster Explain
the Real Issues of the Campaign.
(No Exaggeration or Hearsay)

Webster's Qualifications,
Experience and Education

° ° ° 7 years of college with business administration degree
(tribal president is top administrator and should have
training and knowledge in administration).

°°° 19 years of working with people. Understands Lakota and English very well.
°°° Airborne infantry officer in Korea. 12 years as National Guard officer.
°°° Has served on county, state, and national committees and boards.

Mitakuepi:
Iyuha hupo na wonagon Wasteste nagonpo na nakun Wahanpi Yatkanpo.
Pilamayaya pelo.

> Stanley Red Bird, Chairman
> Poor People's Campaign for Two Hawk

THE INTELLECTUAL TRIBAL LEADER, AS A SOCIAL TYPE

by Margaret Oberly

"We never elect our wisest people to office," said an Eskimo leader. "We elect people who understand your government and whom you understand. Our wisest people have to stay in the villages where we need them." In the course of the myriad meetings and conferences that occupy elected tribal officials, a new type of skilled, professional Indian leader has emerged. (Pamphlet, *Clyde Warrior Institute in American Indian Studies,* undated.)

This type of tribal leader is prevalent today, and I therefore expose him because of the possibility that, in our future, tribal councils there will sit only "The Intellectual Tribal Leader."

His background shows that he received tribal money to attend college for five years—including summer school. Having finally earned his bachelor's degree in elementary education or art, he returns home just brimming with new ideas for the "old Indians back home." So, with his smooth hand on his chinny-chin-chin, and a know-it-all smirk, he views the same tribal council which appropriated funds for college students with utter contempt. Even so, somehow he feels a shred of hope, and therefore he will permit himself to step down to the tribal council in order to lift them out of the scum. Besides, he kinda enjoys all the admiration given an Indian who "made it" through college.

The reason he was chosen is the Indian people's good faith in education. As many of my own elders have put it, "Get an education, learning is good." I will discuss this no further, except to say that this is a widely-held opinion of people who did not have opportunities for education.

Back to the "Intellectual." This man will usually have the support of a newspaper, a school board, a BIA agency official, the local police force, and his pitiful 98 lb. white wife or his overpowering 190 lb. five-foot white wife. The reasons for this support: 1. He will say what white people want to hear. Example: While sitting with the local school board, the question of free hot lunches for the Indian children is raised. At the very mention of this, he replies, making a joke of the whole matter (HA-HA—embarrassed laughter), "No, no, we don't want free lunches. We'll just continue to bring our steak sandwiches in our sacks. (HA-HA—more embarrassed laughter)" 2. His most competent ability to make deals, gentlemen's agreements. Example: He will happily give the right of way to any project that would involve Indian land for the welfare of the nearest town, in order to get the approval of the citizens of that town. His gentlemen's agreement might completely rape an entire reservation, but he would remind you that, "In the long run, it is best for all." Anyway, the mayor shook his hand and the sheriff slapped his left shoulder (after a quick goose), and what more could he ask for?

Need I go on? You can very well understand that this man lives for this type of approval, and he will do anything for it. He would sell your land; take your water rights, your hunting and fishing rights; and, yes, he would even teach your children the great white philosophy. He would also be opposed to passing any legislation which would in effect provide any income for the people, individually or as a whole tribe, because he believes any capital coming from the government to be a "handout."

In conclusion, how can this man be detected? You can usually hear him refer to an old multi-toned car which has no hood, no headlights, three broken windows—one covered with cardboard—tires of different sizes, and sticky, greasy children's fingerprints on the rear view window as . . . a "real Indian Car." He will also refer to the condition of total intoxication as "Indian drunk." In short, he believes everything bad equals everything Indian. Therefore, he would never allow his car to be anything but antiseptically clean and neat.

He believes that there is "a place for everything and everything kept in its place." He will resemble a white man in all mannerisms of dress, speech, and habits. He is sort of a "good imitation of a bad thing," or is it "a bad imitation of a bad thing?" However, his total self-definition adds up to "what he does he is." And, in order to be good and free from filth, sin, poverty, etc., he must do what his definition of good is, which is, "What's white is right and there ain't no kinda room for red, brown, black, or slightly beige."

There you have my definition of the intellectual tribal

leader . . . "learned man" . . . who doesn't know anything.

WHITE IS RIGHT

BLACK IS BEAUTIFUL

RED IS SHORE GOOT-ONE!

▲▲▲▲▲▲▲▲▲▲▲▲▲▲▲▲▲▲▲▲▲▲▲▲▲▲▲▲▲

VI. THE RITUAL OF DEATH: WAR AND PEACE

A DEATH IN SOUTH DAKOTA

> On a ranch in the foothills of the Black Hills, in the autumn of 1969, a white rancher shot a Lakota cowhand. He left the Indian to die in the corral. The local jury acquitted the rancher. Incensed because that year a Lakota university student who had killed a white man was sentenced to death, the urban Indians of the Rapid City (South Dakota) Indian Steering Committee issued this angry proclamation. (Letter to the editor, *Rosebud Sioux Herald,* Rosebud, S.D., Oct. 20, 1969.)

As Indians, we have grown accustomed to the normal amount of bigotry and hypocrisy indigenous to this white Christian republic thickening to an empire.

However, we are not cynical enough yet about your great white nation to be undisturbed by the latest, and most blatant, example of racism in your halls of "justice."

The facts of the case are simple. A man, who is unarmed, walks towards another man and is shot twice and left to die in a corral.

When the man with the gun is a white South Dakotan and the dead man is an Indian, it's known as justifiable homicide.

The only good Indian is a dead Indian, you know.

Well, unfortunately, all the Indians aren't dead so you still have what is known, to the WASP society, as an "Indian problem."

We would argue (and blacks, Mexican-Americans, and Vietnamese would probably agree) that the world has a "white problem."

Since two-thirds of the world is peopled by our dark brothers and sisters, we know that we will eventually solve it.

Oh, by the way, we'll invite you for turkey on Thanksgiving after we've fulfilled our "manifest destiny."

THE CASE OF THOMAS JAMES WHITE HAWK

He was a "white Indian." Gerald Vizenor, in his *Thomas James White Hawk*, wrote of him: "Handsome. Pleasant. Verbal. A most unusual Indian. White Hawk was a beauty mark." As a boy he was orphaned, brought up by the principal of a church mission school on a Sioux reservation in South Dakota. He later became an honors student, the leader of his ROTC platoon, an athletic hero in football, track, and basketball; he won a scholarship to the University of South Dakota. One spring day, in 1967, he murdered a small-town jeweler and raped his wife, for no apparent reason. He pleaded guilty and was sentenced to die in the electric chair. A clemency campaign "saved" his life, but stirred up the *Angst* of his Lakota tribesmen. ("Why Did He Do It?," *City Smoke Signals*, Rapid City, S.D., Feb., 1969.) While in prison, Thomas James White Hawk wrote a short statement incorporating the words of Socrates, whom he admired. ("On Death Row," by Thomas James White Hawk, from Gerald Vizenor, *Thomas James White Hawk*, Mound, Minn., Four Winds Press, 1968.)

Why Did He Do It?

This first paragraph will not relate directly to the subject to be discussed, but it is felt by this writer that the point needs to be made that THOMAS JAMES WHITE HAWK DID NOT HAVE A TRIAL—HE WAS PLED GUILTY BY HIS ATTORNEY AND SENTENCED TO DEATH.

The question has repeatedly been asked, "Why did Tom commit his crime?" I would like to offer a reason, a reason which makes society guilty of this crime and not Tom. However, society has the tendency to want to murder and bury its mistakes rather than accept its responsibility, abolishing capital punishment and creating a situation where a person like Tom can contribute to society.

I would like to remind the reader of the contributions made by the "Birdman of Alcatraz," a convicted murderer whose sentence was commuted to life. He became one of the world's foremost ornithologists and discovered many cures for diseases afflicting birds today. Couldn't Tom do as much if he lives?

Why does someone commit murder? From several years of exposure to the activities of young Indian people, one thing appears to be consistent in their acting out and subsequent committing of offenses, in this case murder.

It appears as if people, as they face the destruction of the social sanctions and other inhibitors set up by their society (in this case the white missionaries and federal government destroying Indian culture), begin to' adopt the dominant group's sanctions. In this process, they face rejection because of racial prejudice. This tends to drive the minorities' sanctions underground or make them non-functional. The best that can happen is that these traits operate only partially.

What happens then, when situations arouse an individual to anger? There is a need to strike out because of the frustration resulting from racial prejudice and discrimination. The individual is no longer controlled by those social sanctions which control most people under normal circumstances and he reacts unshackled.

The psychiatrists in this case testified, as I recall, that Tom was capable of committing this offense and others without feeling guilt, the inference being without conscience. Conscience is a culturally imposed inhibitor on peoples' actions, so if in the mix-up of growing up in two worlds, the individual is not left with strong enough controls, it enables him, it would appear, to react without the restraints placed on people in normal society. The result, murder or whatever.

This situation tends to prevail among urban Indian people. The more young Indian people are torn from Indian society or culture and rejected by the non-Indian, the higher the tendency for crime. Those young people raised in more traditional families experience little or no trouble in adjustment and therefore a low tendency to crime.

This appears to me as a possible explanation for what Tom did. The reader must determine whether or not Tom's life fits into this situation.

On Death Row

Many contemporary people raise the question: How can one both behave in an unrestrained way and at the same time believe correctly that such behavior is wrong? Some people deny that it is possible to do this knowingly. As Socrates thought, it is monstrous, at a time when knowledge is actually present, for anything else to be in charge, dragging knowledge around like a slave. Socrates used to argue wholeheartedly against such a view, his idea being that there is no such thing as lack of restraint, since no one could or would knowingly act contrary to the good. That could only happen through ignorance.

This theory is obviously at variance with plain fact. We must examine the failing more closely, and see if it happens through ignorance—what sort of ignorance this is!

It is clear that the unrestrained man does not think it right to do what he does until he is actually "out of control."

Some thinkers allow part of this, but not all of it. They agree with the view that nothing can be superior to knowledge, but not with the view that no one acts contrary to what, in his opinion, is the best. For this reason, they say that the unrestrained man, when he comes under the influence of pleasure, does not have knowledge; he has opinions instead. But, if it is opinion, and not knowledge, and if the opposing idea is not strong, but weak (as happens with people who are of two minds), it is an understandable fault to stick to such ideas in the face of powerful desires.

> Thomas James White Hawk
> Clay County Jail
> Vermillion, South Dakota
> Summer, 1967

MANIFEST DESTINY: VIETNAM AND THE INDIANS

by Parmenton Decorah

In the white man's conquest of the American West, one out of every three, or four, Indians was exterminated. When Columbus was welcomed by the natives of the Caribbean, there were thought to have been

800,000 to 1,000,000 Indians on the mainland; by 1900 the census showed a mere 240,000 were left. The "policy of extermination" of Indians was at one time endorsed by President Grant. "Death marches" were common. A few of these scars on our history are examined by Parmenton Decorah, an Indian student at the University of Wisconsin. (*Wisconsin Indian Youth Council Newsletter*, Eau Claire, Wis., Vol VI, No. 1, Nov., 1968, p. 2.)

"Go west, young man," said Horace Greeley and so "they" did. And "they" ended up in Vietnam. As God's chosen people, imbued with "manifest destiny," "they" went toward the setting sun, stomping down insignificant savages on the way. "They" did a lot of cool things while in the process of "manifest destiny." Like "they" purchased the Louisiana Territory in 1803, not from the owners, but from a European government—oddly enough. Owners of the territory— the Cheyenne, Sioux, Osage, Omaha, and other nations— did not receive one cent of the money exchanged in the purchase. The money went to those who endeavored to destroy and exterminate the rightful owners. "They" destroyed the "law and order" within the owner nations by stealing the land. How violent can one get? Alas, "they" now cry out for "law and order" after "they" looted America. Surely, it can't be that "they've" gone to pot. After all, "they're" supposed to be "the melting pot of the world." With things not running so smoothly, it seems like something in "their" pot is warped.

The obscenities of the Vietnam War, now being witnessed by the world, manifest certain things. Everyone hopes it's not their destiny. The war manifests that the same thing that "they" pulled with the American Indian is now being attempted with the Vietnamese. Except this time "they're" more sophisticated about it. The corporate structure that dictates "their" lives fears loss of economic power in the world if Vietnam should go the way of the patriotic National Liberation Front. The fact of the matter is that "they" are trying to supplant the Vietnamese culture with "their" system. Just like "they" did with the Indians. If the Vietnamese succumb to "their" way, "they" see that much more economic power in that corner of the world.

The Vietnamese people are a war-stricken people and rarely have experienced peace and independence in their history. They have had invaders galore breach their national sovereignty. Once it was the Chinese, the French, the Japanese, and look who's there now, making mockery of the American Declaration of Independence by denying them free choice of government.

From an Indian viewpoint, the tragedy about it is that there are Indian boys fighting because of the Selective Service System for the same thing that uprooted their cultures. Some are dying, but not for the equal rights and justice they haven't got at home. Like warriors of the past, they are dying for the hope of their people, the essence of their ways of life, and the integrity of their tribal sovereignties. Needless to say, the Indian people have nothing to gain in Vietnam.

The point to be made is that the Indians *don't* have to take the so-called American "manifest destiny" as their own because it has proven to be harmful to people. To survive the American system, Indians must use the system as a means to their very own ends, their own tribal destinies. This can be done by relinquishing the status of dependence on white society, which can be achieved by establishing stable economic bases within tribal structures. Because independence in a capitalistic system requires economic power, masterminding the economic environment should be the top priority on tribal government agendas. Education in fiscal policy, family budgeting, and consumer reports is a suggestion. Attaining economic independence is a prime prerequisite for the Indian people if they are ever to stand among other responsible men of the world in fulfilling their responsibilities as dictates their own good common sense.

WAR AND PEACE

On the prairies, the warriors "counted coup," by coming as close to an enemy as possible, touching him if they could, without being killed or killing him. Courage counted. Not corpses. In this spirit Indians have fought, and most often volunteered to fight, in all the American nation's wars. The Vietnam War, for the first time, has seen Shoshones and Navajos claim that treaty rights exempted them from the draft; Iroquois bands send their young men to Canada; and Vietnam veterans of the Puget Sound tribes have taken off their uniforms, and have refused to return to Vietnam. Some of these changing attitudes are voiced in: ("Indian Vietnam Sentiment Polled," *City Smoke Signals*, Rapid City, S.D., April, 1968; "A Soldier Must Do Battle," by Clyde Sampson, and "Should Indians Fight in White Man's War?", by Stanley Benally, *Navajo Times*, Window Rock, Az., April 2, 1970, and March 26, 1970; and "Navajo Banished to Reservation," *Maine Indian Newsletter*, Vol. III, No. 10, June, 1969.)

Indian Vietnam Sentiment Polled

Recently, a national public opinion agency asked a group of American Indians what they thought about this country's involvement in the current war.

Twenty percent polled said we should get out of South Vietnam.

Eighty percent polled said we should get out of America.

"A Soldier Must Do Battle"

by Clyde Sampson

Dear Editor [*Navajo Times*]:

It is hoped, however, that commensurate with our advancement in the "white man's world" we do not lose sight of our rich culture in Navajo tradition.

As you know, the "paleface" has taken away (for profit only to themselves) our beautiful trees, our rich natural resources, and many other things of value. But, let them not take away the Navajo in you (for it is all we have left).

An Old Indian once said:

"If I knew for a certainty that a paleface was coming to my small house with a conscious design of doing me good, I would run for my life. A smile and the outstretched hand of friendship by a paleface often is more deadly than a rattlesnake."

Today, for example, the Government took [us] beyond our beautiful Navajoland. "The Far East is now our Far West," they boast. We Navajos have sense enough to ask this question: "How can the Far East be the Far West?"

We Navajo always thought that after the paleface exploited our western land the natural boundary of the U.S.A.

was the Pacific Ocean. Now, the great lesson I wish you to bear in mind, my Indian people, is this.

It is to be remembered from Navajo history that while the great white father in Washington reached for the natural boundary the limits, it provided the paleface with the rationale for all American Indians off the globe of our world.

Keep your eyes open. Continue to work hard and progress for your own needs and comfort, of course. But, also [continue] to think *proudly* Navajo in every step you take through life. Never fight for Government's greed for more land in the Far East.

I well understand the euphemisms regarding the war, inasmuch as a soldier must obey rather than probe into the real economic and political reasons (the "commitments" the U.S. has in Vietnam as well as southeast Asia)—why American youth must win the war.

Although we fight bravely against what is called the "Vietcong"—because it is a soldier's duty never to question his Government's military policy—it is to be remembered that we Navajos were called worse by the paleface warriors who invaded our virgin land in order to control us.

The Vietnamese people are fighting for their national liberation. We Navajo also fought, but, as history shows, we lost.

Of course, if a soldier, we must do battle; that is understood. But, someday in the future, when the U.S. Government is correctly branded by all civilized nations as a war criminal, the soldier cannot solve his conscience by saying that he was only following orders. We are there (Vietnam) and must do what all soldiers (who must follow orders or else) do, namely, kill or be killed; indeed, as all soldiers know from the beginning of time, a war is fought in order to survive.

Our Government is not in Vietnam fighting for any ideals;

they are in Vietnam and Southeast Asia in order to protect economic investments which belong only to the *rich*.

The audacity of the U.S. Government who say they are in Asia and Vietnam to stay! The audacity of the U.S. Government when they say to these Americans back home that they cannot afford to lose Vietnam to the communists! Every thinking person should ask themselves, "Who gave Vietnam to *us* to lose?"

So the Vietnamese choose communism; so what? It is their country, not ours. They are fighting for their national independence.

Should Indians Fight in White Man's War?

by Stanley Benally

To the Editor [*Navajo Times*]:

Aside from the tremendous load here at Yale University, I would like to spare this moment to write this letter.

"Grandfathers, should we pick up our rifles again?" My people, I would like to ask you a question. "Why are we fighting the white men's war?" You might answer, "To contain communist aggression and keep world peace." Yes, it is quite true, but why are we fighting in a foreign country, or fighting for what was once ours, to protect what is no longer ours? Once free to roam this peaceful countryside, now confined to only a couple thousand acres of reservation land. This is what my people should be fighting for nonviolently: Against internal corruption and the unethical utilization of white businessmen and many more unsolved problems.

Haphazardly, young Navajo men join Uncle Sam's imperialistic society and find themselves in limbo, somewhere in the midst of mosquito-infested foxholes or on training

grounds. Some go voluntarily, others go involuntarily. . . .
Why? Is it that we want personal glory and to be a hero, or
just to escape from life's miseries?

A yellow, lowdown, cowardly Navajo you may think
about me, but you are wrong. *As a man,* I look at this Vietnam conflict as a senseless war in which Americans have
been fighting the Vietnamese for over fifteen years. In 1954,
when the French were trying to keep Vietnam a French colony, the United States paid 80 percent of the bill. Today,
the fight for United States control of Vietnam continues at a
cost of 30 billion dollars with more than 45,000 Americans
killed. Among the 45,000 killed, Navajos added on to the
figure. *As a Navajo,* I look at war as if fighting alongside the
white man, who tried desperately to annihilate the American Indians (Navajo), fighting for what was once ours and
now to protect what is no longer ours. Last, but not least,
breaking the Navajo's Magna Carta with the United States
government.

Sympathy and worries you leave behind for your parents
and loved ones to cope with. Instantaneous transition takes
place and many find their ego dodging sniper bullets and
struggling to remain alive. Our grandfathers did this, but
with reasons for dodging bullets and struggling to remain
alive. Consequently, our grandfathers were confined to mis-
ery for four long years.

Now I ask you, my people . . . "Will this infamy of the
Vietnam War benefit the Navajo's economical progress?"
The answer is no. Let me take, for example, this Korean
War veteran Dennis Hosteen, and I quote. "Today as I sit at
home without a job I think of those innocents in the Vietnam War that will be returning home soon, saying 'What's
our benefit?' to their fathers, mothers, husbands, wives, children, and friends. For us poor Indians there are none on our
reservation." I definitely agreed with this man because it is

hard to find a job even during the summer, but it would be much harder for the veterans, because all their financial reliabilities will be gone; besides, the Tribe's income will one day disappear because the very limited in the natural resources due to the climatic surroundings. As a result, many will leave the reservation and try to look for jobs in large cities, forgetting that they are Navajo and that there is a reservation. When this transition occurs, only the less fortunate ones will be left behind in poverty.

I believe that the only solution to this problem would be to educate the youths at a college level and try to solve the problems of the Navajo people. I think at the present date there are about 38% or even less that hold a college degree and yet are not doing anything to better the living standards on the reservation, but are too busy trying to develop their financial status and competing with the Jones's. What we need on the reservation are youths with determination to open the doors to real progress of the Navajo Nation.

I might have gotten off on a tangent on the Vietnam War, but I still believe that the Indians have no right whatsoever to fight in any wars, due chiefly to the treaties with the United States government.

After receiving my draft classification I was approached by a law student asking me if Indians had the right to register with the draft board. He then told me that the Indians did not have to register nor have the right to fight in any wars because of the treaties forbidding the Indians to pick up another weapon against their foes. This is why I headed this, "Grandfathers, should we pick up our rifles again?" Also, do we have the right to fight alongside the white man?

Navajo Banished to Reservation

Federal Judge Lloyd Burke sentenced a young Navajo Indian, Donald H. Bitsie, to spend five years on a tribal reservation because he refused to accept the draft laws. Mr.
Bitsie claims that he is exempt from the draft because of the
Treaty signed between Whites and Indians in 1869. It
reads: "They [Navajos] will never kill or scalp White men
nor attempt to do them harm."

Judge Burke gave Bitsie the choice of spending two years
in jail or five years' suspended sentence on a Navajo Reservation.

"I CHOOSE TO SERVE MY PEOPLE": THE STATEMENT OF A VIETNAM VETERAN

by Pvt. Sidney Mills

> Private Sidney Mills is a decorated combat veteran.
> He was "critically wounded" in Vietnam and was
> awarded the Purple Heart. While on leave among his
> tribesmen, in Washington State in the late 1960's, the
> young Indian soldier joined with several other veterans
> in the fish-ins—the tribal demonstrations for their
> treaty fishing rights that have taken place on the rivers
> that empty into Puget Sound since 1964. He "re-
> signed" from the U.S. Army, took off his uniform, and
> decided "to commit [his] life to the Indian people."
> (*Renegade,* published by Survival of American Indian
> Association, Nisqually, Wash., Vol. I, No. 1, May,
> 1969.)

I am a Yakima and Cherokee Indian, and a man. For two
years and four months, I've been a soldier in the United

States Army. I served in combat in Vietnam—until critically wounded. I recently made a decision and publicly declare it today—a decision of conscience, of commitment and allegiance.

I owe and swear first allegiance to Indian people in the sovereign rights of our many Tribes. Owing to this allegiance and the commitment it now draws me to, I hereby renounce future obligation in service or duty to the United States Army.

My first obligation now lies with the Indian people fighting for the lawful Treaty Right to fish in usual and accustomed waters of the Nisqually, Columbia, and other rivers of the Pacific Northwest, and in serving them in this fight in any way possible.

This fight is real—as is the threat to Indian existence under the enforced policy objectives of the State of Washington, as permitted by the compromised position and abdication of responsibilities by the U.S. Government.

The defense of Indian people and a chosen way of life in this fight for unrelinquished fishing rights is more compelling and more demanding of my time and commitment than any duty to the U.S. military. I renounce, and no longer consider myself under, the authorities and jurisdiction of the U.S. Army.

I have served the United States in a less compelling struggle in Vietnam and will not be restricted from doing less for my people within the United States.

The U.S. would have accepted sacrifice of my life in Vietnam in a less legitimate cause—in fact, nearly secured such sacrifice and would have honored such death. Yet, I have my life and am now prepared to stand in another battle, a cause to which the United States owes its protection—a fight for people whom the United States has instead abandoned. My action is taken with the knowledge that the Nation that would have accepted an "honored death" by its requirements may now offer only severe consequence and punishment because I now choose to commit my life to the Indian people.

I have given enough to the U.S. Army—I choose now to serve my people. . . .

This consideration, as much as any, gives immediacy to my decision and prompts me to act upon it now. I will not be among those who draw pride from a past in which I had no part nor from a "proud heritage" I will not uphold.

We must give of ourselves today—and I will not be content to have women or children fighting in my stead. At the least, I will be among them—at the least, they will not be alone.

The disturbing question is, "Why must our Indian people fight?"

Is it because the U.S. Constitution, which declares all treaties made to be the supreme law of the land and contradictory state laws void, is almost 200 years old? But treaties are still being made under force of that document. Or, is it because the Indian treaties involved here are slightly more than one hundred? Or is it because the non-Indian population in this area has increased in the last century from 3,900 to more than 3,000,000?

We do not believe that either antiquity in years or numerical superiority in population acts to diminish legitimate rights not granted by this Nation, but rights retained in valid agreements and guaranteed the protection of the United States in their continued existence and exercise.

▲▲▲▲▲▲▲▲▲▲▲▲▲▲▲▲▲▲

VII. THE LONG ROAD

"WE MEET IN A TIME OF DARKNESS": DECLARATION OF THE FIVE COUNTY CHEROKEES

> An old Lakota man said on hearing the term "New Indians": "Hell with the new Indians! There are no new Indians. There may be old Indians in a new way. And new Indians in an old way. But an Indian is always an Indian." That is the meaning of this message of the traditional councils of the Cherokee in the hills of the Ozarks, which, in the early 1960's, helped light the way of the "New Indian" movements. (*We Meet in a Time of Darkness*, issued by the Councils of the Five County Cherokees, Eastern Oklahoma, undated.)

We, the Five County Cherokees, are one people. We stand united in the sight of God, our Creator. We are joined by love and concern for each other and for all men. . . .

These are our purposes:

We offer ourselves as the voice of the Cherokee people. For many years our people have not spoken and have not been heard. We Cherokees have always known that a free people speak, both with the voice of the whole people and with the voice of each individual person. Among Cherokees, each man has his own way of thinking. We have always had many different organizations, each doing important things. We do not speak as a people until we can speak for every single Cherokee and every single organization. We leave each man and each organization among us free to do their proper job without hindrance or interference. When one Cherokee raises his voice, all Cherokees listen. Since the beginning of time, that has been the Cherokee way. Now we gather as brothers and sisters. We bring with us the belief and the opinions of each of our faiths and organizations. This is how we must speak out as one people. This way we will be listened to.

The Five County Cherokees are the Cherokees of Adair, Cherokee, Delaware, Mayes, and Sequoyah Counties. We meet in a time of darkness to seek the path to the light. We come together, just as our fathers have always done, to do these things:

We ask those among us who are strong and educated to serve us, without pay and with humbleness, as officers and committeemen.

We ask our committeemen and officers to seek the answers to our questions.

We expect them to teach every one of us the answers they find.

We use our right to freedom of speech. This right is the ancient custom of our people. This right is guaranteed by the Constitution of the United States of America. We insist on equality under the laws of these United States. We act now, peaceably but firmly, to carry out the wish of our people.

We will work to establish and to defend those human rights given us by God in our Creation, protected by all our fathers did for us, and insured by the Constitution of the United States of America.

We do this for the benefit of all Cherokees. We do this as a good example to all men. Already we have gathered to protect our rights to harvest fish and game to feed ourselves and our children. From this beginning we will go on until the job is done. We will go on until our lands and our homes are safe. Until we live within the full and just protection of the law. Until we live as the American authors of the Constitution and the Declaration of Independence intended each of the nationalities in this country to live. As dignified men. As free men. As men equal to all other men.

We know the place of Cherokees in this world. For hundreds of years, we ruled ourselves in peace and harmony. Our government was never one man, or a few men. Our government is all our people united. We spoke with wisdom and dignity to our fellow men. We learned of the world around us and made good use of its gifts. We taught people what we knew, while they taught us. For this we are called civilized.

Now, we shall not rest until we have regained our rightful place. We shall tell our young people what we know. We shall send them to the corners of the earth to learn more. They shall lead us.

Now, we have much to do. When our task is done, we will be ready to rest.

In these days, intruders, named without our consent, speak for the Cherokees. When the Cherokee government is the Cherokee people, we shall rest.

In these days, we are informed of the decisions other people have made about our destiny. When we control our own destiny, we shall rest.

In these days, the high courts of the United States listen to people who have been wronged. When our wrongs have been judged in these courts, and the illegalities of the past have been corrected, we shall rest.

In these days, there are countless ways by which people make their grievances known to all Americans. When we have learned these new ways that bring strength and power, and have used them, we shall rest.

In these days, we are losing our homes and our children's homes. When our homeland is protected, for ourselves and for the generations to follow, we shall rest.

In the vision of our Creator, we declare ourselves ready to stand proudly among the nationalities of these United States of America.

THE VOICE OF THE AMERICAN INDIAN, DECLARATION OF INDIAN PURPOSE, AMERICAN INDIAN CHICAGO CONFERENCE

In the summer of 1961, nearly five hundred tribal and urban Indian leaders gathered at the American Indian Chicago Conference. Under the aegis of a group of anthropologists led by Dr. Sol Tax of the University of Chicago and editor of *Current Anthropology*, the conference marked the emergence of the new Indian movement. The young university Indians attending organized to "take over" the conference and go on to found the National Indian Youth Council. (*The Voice of the American Indian*, American Indian Chicago Conference, Conference papers, University of Chicago, June 13–20, 1961.)

Creed

1.   WE BELIEVE in the inherent right of all people to retain spiritual and cultural values and that the free exercise of these values is necessary to the normal development of any people. Indians exercised this inherent right to live their own lives for thousands of years before the white man came and took their lands. It is a more complex world in which Indians live today, but the Indian people who first settled the New World and built the great civilizations which only

now are being dug out of the past long ago demonstrated that they could master complexity.

2. WE BELIEVE that the history and development of America show that the Indian has been subjected to duress, stifling influence, unwarranted pressures, and self-destroying policies which have produced uncertainty, frustration, and despair. Only when the public understands these conditions and is moved to take action toward the formulation and adoption of sound and consistent policies and programs will these destroying factors be removed and the Indian resume his normal growth and make his maximum contribution to modern society.

3. WE BELIEVE in the future of a greater America, an America which we were the first to love, where life, liberty, and the pursuit of happiness will be a reality. In such a future, with Indians and all other Americans co-operating, a cultural climate will be created in which the Indian people will grow and develop as members of a free society.

Statement of Purpose

We, the majority of the Indian People of the United States of America, by compact between equal parties, having the inherent right of self-government, and possessing the same right of sovereignty to voice opinions and desires, do submit a statement of our beliefs:

Therefore: To give recognition to certain basic philosophies by which the Indian People live, WE, the Indian People must be governed by principles in a democratic manner with a right to choose our way of life. Since our Indian culture is threatened by presumption of being absorbed by the American society, we believe we have the responsibility of preserving our precious heritage, recognizing that certain changes are inevitable. We believe that the Indians must provide the adjustment and thus freely advance with dignity to a better life. In order to accomplish the general objectives of the creed adopted at this conference, we the Indian People herein assembled adopt as official the report herewith attached this date, June 19, 1961.

Concluding Statement

To complete our Declaration, we point out that, in the beginning, the people of the New World, called Indians by accident of geography, were possessed of a continent and a way of life. In the course of many lifetimes, our people had adjusted to every climate and condition from the Arctic to the torrid zones. In their livelihood and family relationships, their ceremonial observances, they reflected the diversity of the physical world they occupied.

The conditions in which Indians live today reflect a world in which every basic aspect of life has been transformed. Even the physical world is no longer the controlling factor in determining where and under what conditions men may live. In region after region, Indian groups found their means of existence either totally destroyed or materially modified. Newly introduced diseases swept away or reduced regional populations. These changes were followed by major shifts in the internal life of tribe and family.

The time came when the Indian people were no longer the masters of their situation. Their life-ways survived subject to the will of a dominant sovereign power. This is said not in a spirit of complaint; we understand that, in the lives of all nations of people, there are times of plenty and times of famine. But we do speak out in a plea for understanding.

When we go before the American people, as we do in this Declaration, and ask for material assistance in developing our resources and developing our opportunities, we pose a moral problem which cannot be left unanswered. For the problem we raise affects the standing which our nation sustains before world opinion.

Our situation cannot be relieved by appropriated funds alone, though it is equally obvious that without capital investment and funded services, solutions will be delayed. Nor will the passage of time lessen the complexities which beset a people moving toward new meaning and purpose.

The answers we seek are not commodities to be purchased, neither are they evolved automatically through the passing of time.

The effort to place social adjustment on a money-time interval scale which has characterized Indian administration has resulted in unwanted pressure and frustration.

When Indians speak of the continent they yielded, they are not referring only to the loss of some millions of acres in real estate. They have in mind that the land supported a universe of things they knew, valued, and loved.

With that continent gone, except for the few poor parcels they still retain, the basis of life is precariously held, but they mean to hold the scraps and parcels as earnestly as any small nation or ethnic group was ever determined to hold to identity and survival.

What we ask of America is not charity, not paternalism, even when benevolent. We ask only that the nature of our situation be recognized and made the basis of policy and action.

In short, the Indians ask for assistance, technical and financial, for the time needed, however long that may be, to regain in the America of the space age some measure of the adjustment they enjoyed as the original possessors of their native land.

SELF–DETERMINATION: NATIONAL INDIAN YOUTH COUNCIL STATEMENT OF POLICY

> In the Gallup Indian Community Center (New Mexico), during August, 1961, the youth who had gathered in Chicago earlier that summer founded the National Indian Youth Council. Led by Clyde Warrior (Ponca), Mel Thom (Paiute), and Herbert Blatchford (Navajo), the activist Indian youth participated in the Poor Peoples' March on Washington, D.C., the fish-ins on Puget Sound, the occupation of Alcatraz, and similar movements dedicated to self-determination. (NIYC Statement of Policy, *Indian Truth*, Vol. XLV, No. 3, Winter, 1968–9, p. 10.)

Since earliest contacts with western man, the American Indian has been considered unproductive, unprogressive, and unco-operative. Because we have been classified as a culturally deprived people, we have been subjected to systematic study by foreign cultures, resulting in the imposition of institutions and programs to "improve our condition." Millions of dollars have been poured into projects by the government to help the American Indian; somehow, this money has bypassed the majority of tribal communities and ended up in the pockets of administrators and so-called Indian consultants.

Abandoning a program of militant extermination of the Indian, the government has tried to dictate, through the establishment of colonial structures, the direction of Indian life. Concepts of tribal integrity and cultural equanimity have been overlooked in favor of enculturating the Indian and assimilating him into the American mainstream as fast as possible. The failure of this policy can be evidenced by the existence of 400,000 Indians still living within a tribal system in reservations through the United States. Most of these people live in communities with economic levels well below the poverty criterion. . . . The unwillingness to submit to the government's system of cultural death by allowing oneself to exist under these living standards seems, to us, to be a fight as real as the Indian Wars of the previous century. The weapons employed by the dominant society have become subtler and more dangerous than guns—these, in the form of educational, religious, and social reform, have attacked the very centers of Indian life by attempting to replace native institutions with those of the white man, ignoring the fact that even these native institutions can progress and adapt themselves naturally to the environment.

The major problem in Indian affairs is that the Indian has been neglected in determining the direction of progress and monies to Indian communities. It has always been white people or white-oriented institutions determining what Indian problems are and how to correct them. The Establishment viewpoint has neglected the fact that there are tribal people within these tribal situations who realize the problems and that these people need only the proper social and economic opportunities to establish and govern policies affecting themselves. Our viewpoint, based in a tribal perspective, realizes, literally, that the Indian problem is the white man, and, further, realizes that poverty, educational drop-out, unemployment, etc., reflect only symptoms of a social-contact situation that is directed at unilateral cultural extinction.

Realizing the rise of ethnic consciousness and the dangers of policies directed at that consciousness, the National Indian Youth Council was formed to provide methods of action to protect the tribal communities through the implementation and co-ordination of educational resources. The nature of this work has, basically, been directed into research, training, planning, and programming at community, tribal, and national levels. Believing firmly in the right to self-determination of all peoples, we attempt to reverse the hierarchical structure of existing agencies such that "the People" directly determine the policies of organizations and bureaucracies established to serve them: Therefore, we act as resource individuals to serve our people.

The American Indian has been communicating for the past two centuries; it is time that someone listened. The era of the young Indian as spokesman for his people has, we hope, ended. Realizing that we are of a marginal nature, we are not qualified to act as representatives for a tribal people in voicing, deciding and, judging issues relevant to these people. We are prepared to address our people, not as "potential leaders," but as resources. Leaders arise from the people; an Indian leader cannot be delegated by the BIA or manufactured out of the tribal community by American society through an education that largely ignores his native culture.

APPEAL FOR AN "UNDERDEVELOPED NATION" LOAN

"Self-Determination" and "modernization" were the stated purposes of the "Indian Omnibus Bill," proposed by the administration of President Johnson in 1967. But tribal leaders objected that it merely "entitled" the "tribes [to] mortgage their reservations," and they opposed it. The leaders of thirty major tribes were invited to Washington, D.C., to attend a four-day conference, where government officials, including the Secretary of the Interior, sought to persuade them to endorse the bill. Instead, the tribal leaders rejected the government's pleading and voted 44 to 5 to ask the President for a half-billion-dollar Underdeveloped Nation Loan. (Appeal adopted by Indian delegates attending a special meeting on the proposed "Indian Omnibus Bill" in Washington, D.C., Jan. 30 to Feb. 2, 1967.)

February 2, 1967

We, the representatives of thirty Indian Tribes from ten states, having met for four (4) days in Washington, D.C., at the invitation of the Commissioner of Indian Affairs, to consider the first general legislation in Indian Affairs since the Indian Re-organization Act of 1934, do present this as our recommendation for legislation.

We appreciate the hospitality of the Commissioner of Indian Affairs and his willingness to listen to our views. However, we are unable to regard the proposed legislation under discussion as major legislation or as designed to solve the many pressing problems of poverty on our reservations.

We, therefore, propose to the President, the Congress, and the American people that they take a bold and innovative step. Let them extend to the American Indian people the massive benefits that are now being offered to citizens of the new nations of Asia, Africa, and Latin America. We need technical assistance and development loan funds. We sold our ancestral lands to the United States in return for perpetual protection through federal trusteeship. We do not expect to pay twice.

Instead of the Omnibus Bill, we propose as an alternative that the Federal Government should honor its obligations to the First Americans developing legislation with the following lines:

EDUCATION: The American People are committed to education and American Indian citizens have long been fully committed to education. We desire improved facilities, expanded programs on all levels, and more college and graduate scholarships.

ECONOMIC DEVELOPMENT: We desire an American Indian Development Fund, of a low-interest, long-term nature, comparable to the funds committed to our South American cousins (via the Alliance for Progress) and the native peoples of Africa and Asia. Aid to these peoples totals in excess of $3 billion annually—more than was spent on the American Indian between 1789 and 1960.

To provide prompt rapid economic growth in the underdeveloped areas of our own country, the Indian reservations, we should immediately provide $500 million in loan funds in this proposed fund for economic development of the reservations.

To do less is to deny our own first Americans assistance in social and economic development that we are now already providing others worldwide.

We American Indians are tired of proposals which offer limited assistance and exact as the price the risk of losing our traditional protections afforded by federal trusteeship. We have increasingly good relations with the Bureau of Indian Affairs and are not hampered by present laws and statutes in our community development. However, like any underdeveloped area, we need the capital to develop. Trusteeship by the federal government was the price the United States government paid for this continent and we do not agree to give it up now, nor in the future.

Human and economic development is the essence of trusteeship. Poverty should no longer be its mark or result. The economic development of American Indian tribes and reservations is a special instance of the War on Poverty. We are combatants in that war and we are beginning to win. We are not willing to surrender our role and become passive beneficiaries. We like our relationship with the Bureau of Indian Affairs and see our future in an important relationship. Let us develop a model for the former colonial world and avoid their mistakes.

A Great Society will not willingly or knowingly waste the human and economic resources of its people. Let us continue to develop for the benefit of our Indian people and our country.

RED POWER: AN EIGHT POINT PROGRAM

by the Native Alliance for Red Power

> The demand for "Red Power" was first heard, nationally, at the 23rd Convention of the National Congress of American Indians, held in Oklahoma City, in 1966. It has come to mean different things to different tribes. "Up in Alaska we don't call it [Red Power]," said a Congress vice-president, Eskimo leader William Hendley; "We call it Native Power." In British Columbia, Canada, Indians formed the Native Alliance for Red Power, and issued a definition of what it meant to them in western Canada. ("Red Power: An Eight Point Program," *Akwesasne Notes*, Vol. I, No. 5, May, 1969, p. 47.)

1.   We will not be free until we are able to determine our destiny. Therefore, we want power to determine the destiny of our reservations and communities. Gaining power in our reservations and communities and power over our lives will entail the abolishment of the "Indian Act" and the destruction of the colonial office (Indian Affairs Branch).

2.   This racist government has robbed, cheated, and brutalized us, and is responsible for the deaths of untold numbers

of our people. We feel under no obligation to support this government in the form of taxation. Therefore, we want an end to the collection of money from us in the form of taxes.

3. The history of Canada was written by the oppressors, the invaders of this land. Their lies are perpetrated in the educational system of today. By failing to expose the true history of this decadent Canadian society, the schools facilitate our continued oppression. Therefore, we want an education that teaches us our true history and exposes the racist values of this society.

4. In this country, Indian and Metis represent three percent of the population, yet we constitute approximately sixty percent of the inmates in prisons and jails. Therefore, we want an immediate end to the unjust arrests and harassment of our people by the racist police.

5. When brought before the courts of this country, the red man cannot hope to get a fair hearing from white judges, jurors, and court officials. Therefore, we want natives to be tried by a jury of people chosen from native communities or people of their racial heritage. Also, we want freedom for those of our brothers and sisters now being unjustly held in the prisons of this country.

6. The treaties pertaining to fishing, hunting, trapping, and property rights and special privileges have been broken by this government. In some cases, our people did not engage in treaties with the government and have not been compensated for their loss of land. Therefore, for those of our people who have not made treaties, we want fair compensation. Also, we want the government to honour the statutes, as laid down in these treaties, as being supreme and not to be infringed upon by any legislation whatsoever.

7. The large industrial companies and corporations that have raped the natural resources of this country are responsible, along with their government, for the extermination of the resources upon which we depend for food, clothing and shelter. Therefore, we want an immediate end to this exploitation and compensation from these thieves. We want the government to give foreign aid to the areas comprising the Indian Nation, so that we can start desperately-needed programs concerning housing, agricultural, and industrial cooperatives. We want to develop our remaining resources in the interests of the red man, not in the interests of the white corporate-elite.

8. The white power structure has used every possible method to destroy our spirit and the will to resist. They have divided us into status and non-status, American and Canadian, Metis and Indian. We are fully aware of their "divide and rule" tactic and its effect on our people.

RED POWER IS THE SPIRIT TO RESIST!

RED POWER IS PRIDE IN WHAT WE ARE!

RED POWER IS LOVE FOR OUR PEOPLE!

RED POWER IS OUR COMING-TOGETHER TO FIGHT FOR LIBERATION!

RED POWER IS NOW!

OKLA–HOUMA: THE–RED–EARTH–COLORED– PEOPLE—THE PROGRAM OF THE UNITED NATIVE AMERICANS

> The emergence of Indian "militants" in the late 1960's disturbed the tribal status quo. Elders often complained that their picket lines, sit-ins, and nonviolent protests were "un-Indian." But the United Native Americans, led by Lehman Brightman, a Lakota orator and director of "Indian Studies" at the University of California, soon claimed 5,000 adherents among the college Indian youth and urban Indians, some of whom participated in "militant direct action" such as the occupation of Alcatraz. (United Native Americans, *Warpath*, Vol. I, No. 1, Summer, 1968.)

In California, a completely new kind of organization for the OKLA-HOUMA (Red-earth-colored-people) is being created from the grassroots level—an organization that will seek:

(1) To bring together all people of Indian identity and Indian descent everywhere, not just in the United States, but eventually throughout the Americas;

(2) To bring together all who can identify with the Native American liberation struggle without getting involved in full-blood *vs.* mixed-blood in-fighting or intertribal squabbles (no one who wishes to be a brother is going to be insulted or made fun of because he happens to have only part-Indian biological ancestry—racism is the white man's way, not the Indian's);

(3) To develop chapters everywhere, each chapter being independent at the level of local affairs and all participating democratically in controlling the total organization;

(4) To achieve goals desired by local Indian communities and to respect their heritage and values (we have no room

for either white or brown imperialists who want to cram their own ideas down the throats of local Indian people);

(5) To pull no punches and to do everything possible to achieve justice, economic progress, and political and psychological liberation for Native Americans;

(6) To *not* be controlled by the federal government, by any state governments, or by BIA-run tribal councils, but to be controlled by the Indian people themselves;

(7) To move forward on the basis of *real issues* and to turn our backs on factions, self-serving cliques, "perpetual leadership" groups, and personalism;

(8) To foster a spirit of unity and brotherhood among all Native Americans and to avoid vicious attacks on each other, the objective being to save each misled brother; in other words, to bring every Native American "home" to his people, to not waste one precious Indian life (the white man already destroys enough Indians—why should we destroy each other?);

(9) To work, without compromise, for native control of native affairs at every level;

(10) To do everything possible to aid in the liberation and survival of all native, tribal peoples everywhere.

THE TURTLE ISLAND: THE NORTH AMERICAN INDIAN UNITY CONVENTION

"We follow the sun," once said a contemporary tribal holy man. He referred to the revival of the Indian spirit and religious beliefs throughout the hemisphere, culminating every summer in the "Western Hemisphere Meeting of Indians," or "The North American Indian Unity Convention," led by the Tuscarora prophet Wallace (Mad Bear) Anderson. In 1970, at the meeting "on the land of the Tulalip" (Washington State), this prose poem called the tribes together. (North American Indian Unity Convention, *Indian Magazine*, Healdsburg, Cal., undated.)

While the traffic jams of rush hour continued to clog the cities' streets, and their exhausts to foul the air, the four winds still follow the way of the Great Spirit,

And while bulldozers continued to rape our Mother Earth and loggers to cut our forests, Nature still follows the way of the Great Spirit,

And while dams were being erected across the rivers blocking the return of the spawning fish, the fish still fight to follow the instructions and ways of the Great Spirit,

And while factories and industries were doing their share to pollute our waters, our air, and our land, thus destroying the works of the Great Spirit,

And while people continued their insane dreams for power and riches at the cost of others, of their own brothers, which is not the way of the Great Spirit,

And while the sun was blistering the leaves of trees and turning the grasses yellow across the Great Plains, and shrinking the waters of many lakes and rivers across this turtle island continent of the Great Spirit;

In the month of July, while people turned to the waters to cool themselves of the summer heat;

Apache, Cheyenne, Hopi, Sioux, Mayan, Puyallup, and Nisqually,

Together, as the eagle and the sky,

Tulalip, Eskimo, Umatilla, Pomo, Klamath, Coeur d'Alene, and Quinault,

children of the Great Spirit, we did gather, as the four winds,

Walla Walla, Shoshone, Blackfoot, Paiute, Potawatomi, Mohawk, and Lumbee,

> together we gathered, as brothers and sisters, as the all-ness of nature,

Pitt River, Suswap, Cherokee Nation, Muckleshoot, Snoqualmie, Yakima, and Tuscarora,

> together to form the circle, the hoop, the sacred roundness of all Indian peoples.

Sac and Fox, Omaha, Mescalero, Pima, Onondaga, Iowa, Nootka, Salish, Quechan, Pueblo, Hoopa, Wintun, Algonquin, Seneca, and Cree,

> we came to listen and to speak,

Shusap, Lummi, Tlinget, Penobscot, Comanche, Montagnais, and Stilliguamish,

> there, in the far away land of the northwest, on the shores of the big waters, we met as guests of the Tulalip people.
>
> In the longhouse of the Tulalip, we sat to council;

Kiowa, Warm Springs, Canada Blackfoot and Cree, Samish, Chippewa, Duwamish, and Shawnee,

To council and to listen to the elders of our many tribes,

To hear the prophecies of our traditional people and to share our many common ties,

We the people of the land, the true children of our Earth Mother, because we are the very land,

We met to learn and to bring to light the many problems facing our people,

As our Mother Earth is being destroyed and contaminated, and as the Great Spirit grows angry at this waste and greed,

We met, not to weep over today and yesterday, but to plan and to create a better future for our children,

We met, as guardians of this turtle island continent to renew our strength and courage in the face of all that is evil in this day and age.

"WE HOLD THE ROCK": ALCATRAZ PROCLAMATION TO THE GREAT WHITE FATHER AND HIS PEOPLE

Ignored by the communications media, a group of young Indians occupied the abandoned federal prison of Alcatraz in 1964 to establish an Indian University. They were driven off. Once more, in the fall of 1969, several dozen tribesmen invaded Alcatraz, and formed the Indians of All Nations. Led by Richard Oakes, a Mohawk who directed "Indian Studies" at San Francisco State College, and Grace Thorpe, a Sac and Fox, the daughter of all-time Olympic hero Jim Thorpe, they claimed the island under an old federal law and issued this proclamation. ("We Hold The Rock," *Alcatraz Indians of All Tribes Newsletter*, Vol. I, No. 1, Jan., 1970.)

Fellow citizens, we are asking you to join with us in our attempt to better the lives of all Indian people.

We are on Alcatraz Island to make known to the world that we have a right to use our land for our own benefit.

In a proclamation of November 20, 1969, we told the government of the United States that we are here "to create a meaningful use for our Great Spirit's Land."

We, the native Americans, reclaim the land known as Alcatraz Island in the name of all American Indians by right of discovery.

We wish to be fair and honorable in our dealings with the Caucasian inhabitants of this land, and hereby offer the following treaty:

We will purchase said Alcatraz Island for twenty-four dollars (24) in glass beads and red cloth, a precedent set by the white man's purchase of a similar island about 300 years ago. We know that $24 in trade goods for these 16 acres is more than was paid when Manhattan Island was sold, but we know that land values have risen over the years. Our offer of $1.24 per acre is greater than the 47¢ per acre the white men are now paying the California Indians for their lands.

We will give to the inhabitants of this island° a portion of the land for their own to be held in trust . . . by the Bureau of Caucasian Affairs . . . in perpetuity—for as long as the sun shall rise and the rivers go down to the sea. We will further guide the inhabitants in the proper way of living. We will offer them our religion, our education, our life-ways in order to help them achieve our level of civilization and thus raise them and all their white brothers up from their savage and unhappy state. We offer this treaty in good faith and wish to be fair and honorable in our dealings with all white men.

We feel that this so-called Alcatraz Island is more than suitable for an Indian reservation, as determined by the white man's own standards. By this, we mean that this place resembles most Indian reservations in that:

1. It is isolated from modern facilities, and without adequate means of transportation.
2. It has no fresh running water.
3. It has inadequate sanitation facilities.
4. There are no oil or mineral rights.
5. There is no industry and so unemployment is very great.
6. There are no health-care facilities.
7. The soil is rocky and non-productive, and the land does not support game.

° "This island" refers to the "Turtle Island," which many tribes call the North American continent; and "the inhabitants" refers to the white newcomers [—eds.].

8. There are no educational facilities.
9. The population has always exceeded the land base.
10. The population has always been held as prisoners and kept dependent upon others.

Further, it would be fitting and symbolic that ships from all over the world, entering the Golden Gate, would first see Indian land, and thus be reminded of the true history of this nation. This tiny island would be a symbol of the great lands once ruled by free and noble Indians.

What use will we make of this land?

Since the San Francisco Indian Center burned down, there is no place for Indians to assemble and carry on tribal life here in the white man's city. Therefore, we plan to develop on this island several Indian institutions:

1. A Center for Native American Studies will be developed which will educate them [our people—eds.] to the skills and knowledge relevant to improve the lives and spirits of all Indian peoples. Attached to this center will be traveling universities, managed by Indians, which will go to the Indian Reservations, learning those necessary and relevant materials now about.

2. An American Indian Spiritual Center, which will practice our ancient tribal religious and sacred healing ceremonies. Our cultural arts will be featured and our young people trained in music, dance, and healing rituals.

3. An Indian Center of Ecology, which will train and support our young people in scientific research and practice to restore our lands and waters to their pure and natural state. We will work to de-pollute the air and waters of the Bay Area. We will seek to restore fish and animal life to the area and to revitalize sea-life which has been threatened by the white man's way. We will set up facilities to desalt sea water for human benefit.

4. A Great Indian Training School will be developed to teach our people how to make a living in the world, improve our standard of living, and to end hunger and unemployment among all our people. This training school will include a center for Indian arts and crafts, and an Indian restaurant serving native foods, which will restore Indian culinary arts. This center will display Indian arts and offer Indian foods to the public, so that all may know of the beauty and spirit of the traditional Indian ways.

Some of the present buildings will be taken over to develop an American Indian Museum which will depict our native food and other cultural contributions we have given to the world. Another part of the museum will present some of the things the white man has given to the Indians in return for the land and life he took: disease, alcohol, poverty, and cultural decimation (as symbolized by old tin cans, barbed wire, rubber tires, plastic containers, etc.). Part of the museum will remain a dungeon to symbolize both those Indian captives who were incarcerated for challenging white authority and those who were imprisoned on reservations. The museum will show the noble and tragic events of Indian history, including the broken treaties, the documentary of the Trail of Tears, the Massacre of Wounded Knee, as well as the victory over Yellow-Hair Custer and his army.

In the name of all Indians, therefore, we reclaim this island for our Indian nations, for all these reasons. We feel this claim is just and proper, and that this land should rightfully be granted to us for as long as the rivers run and the sun shall shine.

We hold the Rock!

VIII. PROPHECIES OF THE FUTURE

"WHERE DO WE STAND TODAY?":
THE HOPI PROPHECY UPDATED

> The prophecies which have emerged from the tribal
> past, like underground streams, nourish the modern
> Indian movements. Of these ancient visions that fore-
> tell the future, none is better known, nor more influen-
> tial, than the Hopi Prophecy. It was the source of the
> "Letter to President Truman" by the Hopi clan chiefs
> and traditional leaders who challenged the U.S. gov-
> ernment's moral authority and reaffirmed their own re-
> ligious beliefs. "What has become of your religion?"
> the Hopis asked the President. (*Letter to President
> Truman*, Hopi Nation, Az., privately published, 1949.)

Hopi Indian Empire
Oraibi, Arizona
March 28, 1949

The President
The White House
Washington, D.C.

To the President:

We, the hereditary Hopi Chieftains of the Hopi Pueblos
of Hotevila, Shungopovi, and Mushongnovi humbly request
a word with you.

Thoroughly acquainted with the wisdom and knowledge
of our traditional form of government and our religious prin-

ciples; sacredly authorized and entrusted to speak, act, and to execute our duties and obligations for all the common people throughout this land of the Hopi Empire, in accordance with the fundamental principles of life, which were laid down for us by our Great Spirit, Masau'u, and by our forefathers, we hereby assembled in the Hopi Pueblo of Shungopovi on March 9, 13, 26, and 28 of this year 1949 for the purpose of making known to the government of the United States and others in this land that the Hopi Empire is still in existence, its traditional path unbroken and its religious order intact and practiced, and the Stone Tablets, upon which are written the boundaries of the Hopi Empire, are still in the hands of the Chiefs of Oraibi and Hotevila Pueblos. . . .

What we say is from our hearts. We speak truths that are based upon our own tradition and religion. We speak as the first people in this land you call America. And we speak to you, a white man, the last people who came to our shores seeking freedom of worship, speech, assembly, and a right to life, liberty, and the pursuit of happiness. And we are speaking to all the American Indian people.

Today we, Hopi and white man, come face to face at the crossroad of our respective life. At last our paths have crossed and it was foretold it would be at the most critical time in the history of mankind. Everywhere, people are confused. What we decide now and do hereafter will be the fate of our respective people. Because we Hopi leaders are following our traditional instructions, we must make our position clear to you and we expect you to do the same to us. . . .

The Hopi form of government was established solely upon religious and traditional grounds. The divine plan of life in this land was laid out for us by Great Spirit, Masau'u. This plan cannot be changed. The Hopi life is all set according to the fundamental principles of life of this divine plan. We can not do otherwise but to follow this plan. There is no other way for us. . . .

This land is a sacred home of the Hopi people and all the Indian race in this land. It was given to the Hopi people the task to guard this land not by force of arms, not by killing, not by confiscating of properties of others, but by humble prayers, by obedience to our traditional and religious instructions, and by being faithful to our Great Spirit, Masau'u. We are still a sovereign nation. Our flag still flies throughout our land (our ancient ruins). We have never abandoned our sovereignty to any foreign power or nation. We've been self-governing people long before any white man came to our shores. What Great Spirit made and planned no power on earth can change.

The boundaries of our Empire were established permanently and was written upon Stone Tablets which are still with us. Another was given to his white brother, who after emerging of the first people to this new land went east with the understanding that he will return with his Stone Tablet to the Hopis. These Stone Tablets when put together and if they agree will prove to the whole world that this land truly belongs to the Hopi people and that they are true brothers. Then the white brother will restore order and judge all people here who have been faithful to their traditional and religious principles and who have mistreated his people. . . .

We, the traditional leaders, want you and the American people to know that we will stand firmly upon our own traditional and religious grounds. And that we will not bind ourselves to any foreign nation at this time. Neither will we go with you on a wild and reckless adventure which we know will lead us only to a total ruin. Our Hopi form of government is all set and ready for such eventuality. We have met all other rich and powerful nations who have come to

our shores, from the Early Spanish Conquistadors down to
the present government of the United States, all of whom
have used force in trying to wipe out our existence here in
our own home. We want to come to our own destiny in our
own way. We have no enemy. We will neither show our
bows and arrows to anyone at this time. This is our only way
to everlasting life and happiness. Our tradition and religious
training forbid us to harm, kill and molest anyone. We,
therefore, objected to our boys being forced to be trained
for war to become murderers and destroyers. It is you who
should protect us. What nation who has taken up arms ever
brought peace and happiness to his people?

All the laws under the Constitution of the United States
were made without our consent, knowledge, and approval,
yet we are being forced to do everything that we know is
contrary to our religious principles and those principles of
the Constitution of the United States.

Now we ask you, American people, what has become of
your religion and your tradition? Where do we stand today?
The time has come now for all of us as leaders of our people
to re-examine ourselves, our past deeds, and our future
plans. The judgment day will soon be upon us. Let us make
haste and set our house in order before it is too late.

We believe these to be truths, and from our hearts and
for these reasons, we, Hopi Chieftains, urge you to give
these thoughts your most earnest considerations. And after a
thorough and careful consideration, we want to hear from
you at your earliest convenience. This is our sacred duty to
our people. We are,

Sincerely yours,

Chief Talahaftewa, Village Chief, Bear Clan, Shungopovi
Basevaya, Adviser, Katchin Clan, Shungopovi
Andrew Hermequaftewa, Adviser, Blue Bird Clan, Shungo-
povi

Chief Sackmasa, Village Crier, Coyote Clan, Mushongnovi
Chief James Pongayawyma, Village Chief, Kokop Clan
(Fire), Hotevila
Chief Dan Katchongva, Adviser, Co-ruler, Sun Clan, Hotev-
ila

THE LOST BROTHER:
AN IROQUOIS PROPHECY OF THE SERPENTS

as retold by Wallace (Mad Bear) Anderson

> Deganawidah was a prophet of the Iroquois, who
> came among them of virgin birth when they were war-
> ring tribes hundreds of years ago—the Onondagas,
> Senecas, Oneidas, Cayugas, and Mohawks. And he
> united them. "We bind ourselves together by taking
> hold of each other's hands so firmly and forming a cir-
> cle so strong that if a tree should fall upon it, it could
> not shake nor break it." Later, the Tuscaroras joined
> the circle. And, later still, a young Tuscarora, Wallace
> (Mad Bear) Anderson, a merchant seaman and reli-
> gious activist, in the 1950's retold and revitalized the
> prophecy of Deganawidah by urging the unity of all
> Indians on all continents. (*Apologies to the Iroquois* by
> Edmund Wilson, New York, Farrar, Straus & Giroux,
> 1959, pp. 163–7.)

Sometimes, I feel that the struggle is completely hopeless.
Then, again, I don't know. I think that maybe some day the
Iroquois will come into their own again.

When Deganawidah was leaving the Indians in the Bay of
Quinte in Ontario, he told the Indian people that they
would face a time of great suffering. They would distrust
their leaders and the principles of Peace of the League, and

a great white serpent was to come upon the Iroquois, and for a time it would intermingle with the Indian people and would be accepted by the Indians, who would treat the serpent as a friend. This serpent would, in time, become so powerful that it would attempt to destroy the Indian, and the serpent is described as choking the life's blood out of the Indian people. Deganawidah told the Indians that they would be in such a terrible state at this point that all hope would seem to be lost, and he told them that when things looked their darkest a red serpent would come from the north and approach the white serpent, which would be terrified, and upon seeing the red serpent he would release the Indian, who would fall to the ground almost like a helpless child, and the white serpent would turn all its attention to the red serpent.

The bewilderment would cause the white serpent to accept the red serpent momentarily. The white serpent would be stunned and take part of the red serpent and accept him. Then there is a heated argument and a fight. And then the Indian revives and crawls toward the land of the hilly country, and then he would assemble his people together, and they would renew their faith and the principles of peace that Deganawidah had established. There would at the same time exist among the Indians a great love and forgiveness for his brother, and in this gathering would come streams from all over—not only Iroquois, but from all over—and they would gather in this hilly country, and they would renew their friendship. And Deganawidah said they would remain neutral in this fight between the white serpent and the red serpent.

At the time they were watching the two serpents locked in this battle, a great message would come to them, which would make them ever so humble, and when they become that humble, they will be waiting for a young leader, an Indian boy, possibly in his teens, who would be a choice seer. Nobody knows who he is or where he comes from, but he will be given great power, and would be heard by thousands, and he would give them the guidance and the hope to refrain them from going back to their land and he would be the accepted leader. And Deganawidah said that they will gather in the land of the hilly country, beneath the branches of an elm tree, and they should burn tobacco and call upon Deganawidah by name when we are facing our darkest hours, and he will return. Deganawidah said that as the choice seer speaks to the Indians that number as the blades of grass and he would be heard by all at the same time, and as the Indians are gathered watching the fight, they notice from the south a black serpent coming from the sea, and he is described as dripping with salt water, and as he stands there, he rests for a spell to get his breath, all the time watching to the north to the land where the white serpent and the red serpent are fighting.

Deganawidah said that the battle between the white and the red serpents opened real slow but would then become so violent that the mountains would crack and the rivers would boil and the fish would turn up on their bellies. He said that there would be no leaves on the trees in that area. There would be no grass, and strange bugs and beetles would crawl from the ground and attack both serpents, and he said that a great heat would cause the stench of death to sicken both serpents. And then, as the boy seer is watching this fight, the red serpent reaches around the back of the white serpent and pulls from him a hair which is carried towards the south by a great wind into the waiting hands of the black serpent, and as the black serpent studies this hair, it suddenly turns into a woman, a white woman who tells him things that he knows to be true but he wants to hear them again. When this white woman finishes telling these things, he takes her and gently places her on a rock with great love and respect, and then he becomes infuriated at what he has heard, so he makes a beeline for the north, and he enters the battle between the red and white serpents with such speed and anger that he defeats the two serpents, who have already been battle-weary.

When he finishes, he stands on the chest of the white serpent, and he boasts and puts his chest out like he's the conqueror, and he looks for another serpent to conquer. He looks to the land of the hilly country and then he sees the Indian standing with his arms folded and looking ever so nobly so that he knows that this Indian is not the one that he should fight. The next direction that he will face will be eastward and at that time he will be momentarily blinded by a light that is many times brighter than the sun. The light will be coming from the east to the west over the water, and, when the black serpent regains his sight, he becomes terrified and makes a beeline for the sea. He dips into the sea and swims away in a southerly direction, and shall never again be seen by the Indians. The white serpent revives, and he, too, sees this light, and he makes a feeble attempt to gather himself and go toward that light. A portion of the white serpent refuses to remain, but instead makes its way toward the land of the hilly country, and there he will join the Indian People with a great love like that of a lost brother. The rest of the white serpent would go to the sea and dip into the sea and would be lost out of sight for a spell. Then, suddenly, the white serpent would appear again on the top of the water and he would be slowly swimming toward the light. Deganawidah said that the white serpent would never again be a troublesome spot for the Indian people. The red serpent would revive and he would shiver with great fear when he sees the light. He would crawl to the north and leave a bloody shaky trail northward, and he would never be seen again by the Indians. Deganawidah said as this light approaches that he would be that light, and he would return to his Indian people, and when he returns, the Indian people would be a greater nation than they ever were before.

PROPHECY OF THE FOUR-LEGGED MAN: "WE WILL DEFEAT GOLIATH"

by Reverend Clifton Hill

> In Indian prophecy, the Apocalypse is rarely an Arma-geddon. So, the "Four-Legged Man" (the white man) in the modern vision of Reverend Clifton Hill, which he proclaimed in 1964, will simply "disappear" by the wisdom of God and by man's own destructiveness. A powerfully-built young man, who grew up chopping cotton, a former Golden Gloves boxer, the son of a Baptist minister and himself a Baptist minister, Hill, the leader of the Creek Tribal Centralization Commit-tee (Oklahoma) says he is no prophet. "I see myself as a Robin Hood. That's what we need, a Robin Hood type," he says. (*The New Indians*, pp. 110–12, 115.)

I am not saying I am the Messiah, or the Savior. . . .

The Indian is always looking for a Messiah, or a Savior, to lead him to prosperity. I am just a poor, stupid Indian. . . .

I always tell my people we are like Little David in the Bible. . . .

The Biblical story goes that Israel was fearful of the Phil-istines. These Philistines were giants; they had the powers and authorities. I can hear the giants of this Philistine army saying, "We belong to the Methodist Conference. We be-long to the Southern Baptist Church. We belong to the Bureau of Indian Affairs. We got the power. We got the United States behind us. We can do anything. We can steal and rob and lie—anything."

And here comes Little David, our organization. Poor, but stands for justice. And the Israelites were expecting their Savior to be mighty and strong and intelligent. But God looked around. He saw a little shepherd boy out in the field, just with a little sheep clothing on, a little satchel of pebbles, and a little slingshot on his side. And God said, "I'm going to send you out to deliver your people."

Well, at the great front lines the Israelites were fearful, they were frightened, they were ready to run. They were so shocked and the enemy was so strong, and there was nothing they could do. And Little David, he came on the scene, and he said, "I am the man God sent!" The Israelites said, "Oh, my God! Why in the world did He send something like that? So young and not strong. He couldn't be our Savior."

And Little David, here we see him. They put the helmet on him. He took it off. They put the breastplate on him. He took it off. They wanted him to be connected up with the Bureau of Indian Affairs, or some big Christian movement. And the Israelites were so ashamed, they said, "He couldn't do nothing. There is nothing he could accomplish for us."

But the little shepherd boy he come out of the trench. The Bible tells me that the giant's shadow overshadowed him. And I can hear Little David say, "In the name of the Lord. The Lord is Justice." And as he began to walk in the shadow of the great Philistine the Bible tells me he destroyed him! . . .

Way before 1500, way before the contact of the white man, the elder council used to sit around and prophesy into this age: That a four-legged man would come out of the sea unto this continent, and through his intelligency he would surpass the Indian. He would dominate him. He would strip him of everything. And then he would destroy him. The four-legged man would destroy the Indian almost to nothing.

And the elder council prophesied: When the four-legged man had done all the damage he could he would return back to the sea and disappear. And then the Indian would come back. He would call his children together and teach them and admonish them and they would reconstruct their laws and traditions. And they would live forever. That is the story of what will happen. . . .

I do definitely believe that we will, . . . we will defeat Goliath.

THE WARRIORS OF THE RAINBOW

by William Willoya

> "Peace after the storms of war and suffering, God's covenant with mankind through His Prophets, and the union of all the colors of the races of mankind in pleasing harmony . . ."—this is the symbol of the rainbow. William Willoya, whose vision this is, is an Eskimo. He was a hunter of seals in the Bering Strait before his journeys across the continent, after World War II, seeking out and uniting the prophecies of many tribes in his "New Message" of "the spiritual regeneration and uplifting of all mankind." (*Warriors of the Rainbow*, by William Willoya and Vinson Brown, Healdsburg, Cal., Naturegraph Company, 1952, pp. 77–80.)

We have seen the golden thread of the prophecies that foretell the day of the awakening of the Indian peoples and the formation of a New World of justice and peace, of freedom and God. We have seen how the Warriors of the Rainbow (the new teachers) are prophesied to come and spread this great Message all over the earth. But how are the Indians going to help these prophecies come true?

For long years, the Indian peoples have been sleeping, physically conquered by the white people. For all this time, they have been taught to believe that the white men were superior to them, that they must learn to live in and become a part of this white civilization, as it exists, even if a lowly part. It will not be easy to awaken them from their sleep. It can be done if we realize that the Indians are sleeping giants, that within each of them are marvelous powers of the spirit that need only be started into action to create miracles of work done for the good of all and deeds of shining heroism.

Like the great Indians of old, they will teach unity, love, and understanding among all people. They will listen no more to the little people who say they alone have the truth, but shall see that He Who Listens to All is too big for little things, too full of justice to accept but one self-chosen people, too free to be caged by any mind. They will listen instead to those who teach harmony between all men, even as the wind blows without favoritism into all the corners of the world.

Like the pure Indians of old, they will pray to the Spirit with a love that flows through every world, even as the breeze sings its song to the Silent One among the needles of the pines. . . .

Like the glorious Indians of the past, by their joy, by their laughter, their love, and their understanding, they shall change all men whom they meet. . . .

Like the radiant Indians of old who strengthened their muscles by hard exercise and then nourished their souls by fasting and prayer, so shall they make themselves heroes of the new age, conquering every difficulty with the strength of their bodies, the fire of their love, and the purity of their hearts. . . .

Like the Indians of old who let their children run free in the prairies, the woods, and the mountains to help them grow into men and women worthy of their Creator, so the Warriors of the Rainbow today shall work to bring to all children the magic blessing of the wild, the delight of bare feet running through green grass over the hills, and the cool touch of the wind in their hair. The spiritual civilization that is coming will create beauty by its very breath, turning the waters clear, building forests and parks where there are now deserts and slums, and bringing back the flowers to the hill-sides. What a glorious fight to change the world to beauty!

Like the Indians of old who loved, understood, and knew the power of animals and plants; who killed or took no more than they needed for food or clothing; so the Indians of today will brighten the understanding of the ignorant de-stroyers. They will soften the hearts of would-be killers so that the animals will once more replenish the earth, and the trees shall once more rise to hold the precious soil. . . .

Like the kind Indians of old who gave work to all and kept care of the poor, the sick, and the weak, so the Warri-ors of the Rainbow shall work to build a new world in which everyone who can work shall work and work with joy and with praise of the Great Spirit. None shall starve or be hurt due to the coldness and forgetfulness of men. . . .

Like the joyful Indians of old, the new Indians shall bring back to their own people and spread to other races the joy of good-fellowship and kindness and courtesy that made the life in the old Indian villages such a happy time for all. How they danced together! How they ate together in loving har-mony! How they prayed together and sang together in joy! It shall come again and better in the new world.

Wise Indians do not speak without reason and they shame

a boaster by their silence; so, today, the Indians shall teach all people to make their deeds count bigger than their words. Deeds of love and kindness and understanding shall change the world.

Even as the wise chiefs are chosen, not by political parties, not by loud talks and boasting, not by calling other men names, but by demonstrating always their quiet love and wisdom in council and their courage in making decisions and working for the good of all, so shall the Warriors of the Rainbow teach that, in the governments of the future, men will be chosen out of the ranks by quality alone and then will counsel together in freedom of thought and conscience. In counsel, they shall seek truth and harmony with hearts full of wisdom and prefer their brothers to themselves.

The thoughtful and devoted chiefs of old understood their people with love; the parents of old educated their children with love; all new Indians will associate with other religions and peoples with love. One minute of such love and understanding brings wealth from the Great Spirit and creates miracles of accomplishment. It is love, then, with understanding that the Warriors of the Rainbow will mix in their medicine to heal the world of its ills, leavened with pure hearts and humble minds. . . .

Great are the tasks ahead, terrifying are the mountains of ignorance and hate and prejudice, but the Warriors of the Rainbow shall rise as on the wings of the eagle to surmount all difficulties. They will be happy to find that there are now millions of people all over the earth ready and eager to rise and join them in conquering all barriers that bar the way to a new and glorious world! We have had enough now of talk. Let there be deeds.

"The morning stars sang together, and all the sons of God shouted for joy." *Job*, 38:7.

"SO LET THERE BE HAPPINESS"

Apache tribe

It is good to end with the beginning. An Apache child has told of the creation of the First People, the Apache people, and how they wished to live on earth, in peace. The old story was told in a book of young Indians' thoughts that was symbolically titled, *The New Trail*. (*The New Trail*, Phoenix, Az., the Phoenix Indian School, Bureau of Indian Affairs, 1953.)

As the family of Ba-go-szo-na were sitting, there came toward them the slithering snake, "glish." Meh, the baby, started crawling toward the glish, but Ba-go-szo-na pulled her back and said to the glish:

> *Yo shu la*
> *No he jahu ga do go lah*
> *ta dun teh yah*
> *He ya go da leh*
> *Ah qu ju gohl la*
> *Lua no he queck do le la*
> *Yo shu la*

> So let there be happiness.
> We who live in this encampment
>   here are poor.
> We strive to live by the soil and
>   labor of our hands.
> So be on your way. And do not
>   harm us.
> So let there be happiness.

ACKNOWLEDGMENTS

The editors gratefully acknowledge the following sources:

"The Pretty Colored Snake," from Reverend Watt Spade and Willard Walker, *Cherokee Stories* (Middletown, Connecticut: Wesleyan University, The Laboratory of Anthropology, 1966). Reprinted by permission.

"Restore Us to Our Country," from Louis Thomas Jones, *Aboriginal American Oratory* (Los Angeles: Southwest Museum, 1965). Reprinted by permission.

"As Snow Before a Summer Sun," from *Akwesasne Notes*, Vol. I, No. 5, May, 1969. Published and reprinted by permission of the Mohawk Nation at Akwesasne, Roosevelt, New York.

"Let Our Affairs Be Transacted by Warriors," from Louis Thomas Jones, *Aboriginal American Oratory* (Los Angeles: Southwest Museum, 1965). Reprinted by permission.

"He Drank the Blood of Some Whites," from *Akwesasne Notes*, Vol. I, No. 6, June, 1969. Published and reprinted by permission of the Mohawk Nation at Akwesasne, Roosevelt, New York.

"Our New Home Will Be Beyond a Great River," from Louis Thomas Jones, *Aboriginal American Oratory* (Los Angeles: Southwest Museum, 1965). Reprinted by permission.

"Those Who Made War Against the White Man Always Failed," from Frank B. Linderman, *Plenty-Coups, Chief of the Crows* (Lincoln, Nebraska: University of Nebraska Press, 1962). Copyright 1957 and reprinted by permission of the University of Nebraska Press.

"You Are Like Dogs in the Hot Moon," from Meridel Le Seur, *North*

Star Country (New York: Book Find Club, 1945). Reprinted by permission.

"Dakotas, I Am for War," from Louis Thomas Jones, *Aboriginal American Oratory* (Los Angeles: Southwest Museum, 1965). Reprinted by permission.

"The Day Before the Battle on the Little Big Horn," from *Rosebud Sioux Herald* (*Eyapaha*), Rosebud, South Dakota, October 20, 1969. Reprinted by permission of the author.

"Our People Are Blindly Deceived," from the *Great Plains Observer*, Madison, South Dakota, January, 1969. Reprinted by permission.

"Your People Have Destroyed My Nation," from Louis Thomas Jones, *Aboriginal American Oratory* (Los Angeles: Southwest Museum, 1965). Reprinted by permission.

"Dead, Did I Say? There Is No Death," from Louis Thomas Jones, *Aboriginal American Oratory* (Los Angeles: Southwest Museum, 1965). Reprinted by permission.

"A Word Has Power," from N. Scott Momaday, *The Way to Rainy Mountain* (Albuquerque: University of New Mexico Press, 1969). Reprinted by permission of the author.

"The Mysterious Bird and the Land of Death," from Jaime de Angulo, *Indian Tales* (New York: Hill and Wang, 1953). Reprinted by permission.

"Ceremony for Rain," from Sidney M. Callaway, Gary Witherspoon *et al.*, *Grandfather Stories* (Rough Rock, Arizona: Navajo Curriculum Center, 1970). Reprinted by permission.

"The Legend of Dr. Fewkes and Masauwu," from Edmund Naquatewa, edited by Mary Russell F. Colton, *Truth of the Hopi* (Museum of Northern Arizona, 1967). Reprinted, courtesy of the Museum of Northern Arizona.

"Manabozho and the Gambler," from Gerald Vizenor, *Anishinabe Adisokan* (Minnesota: Nodin Press, 1970). Reprinted by permission of the author.

"What Is an Indian Reservation?" from *Akwesasne Notes*, Vol. I, No. 7,

July, 1969. Published and reprinted by permission of the Mohawk Nation at Akwesasne, Roosevelt, New York.

"We Do Not Want Any Other Home," from Louis Thomas Jones, *Aboriginal American Oratory* (Los Angeles: Southwest Museum, 1965). Reprinted by permission.

"Colonialism: Classic and Internal," by Robert K. Thomas, from *New University Thought*, Vol. IV, No. 4, Winter, 1966–7. Reprinted by permission.

"The Dog Problem," from *Maine Indian Newsletter*, Vol. III, No. 6, February, 1969, Old Town, Maine. Reprinted by permission.

"Always Againsting My Husband Albert Hanois and Everything," from *Maine Indian Newsletter,* Vol. III, No. 3, November, 1968, Old Town, Maine. Reprinted by permission.

"The Speech I Didn't Give," from an unpublished article, reprinted by permission of the author.

"Indians As Human Beings," from *Integrated Education,* Issue 26, Vol. V, No. 2, April–May, 1967, Chicago, Illinois. Reprinted by permission.

"Relocation," from Reverend Watt Spade and Willard Walker, *Cherokee Stories* (Middletown, Connecticut: Wesleyan University, Laboratory of Anthropology, 1966). Reprinted by permission.

"Relocation," "Missing That Indian Name of Roy or Ray," and "West: Grants to Gallup, New Mexico," from *Rough Rock News.* Reprinted by permission of the author.

"The Indian in Suburbia," from *The American Indian,* San Francisco Indian Center, March, 1964. Reprinted by permission.

"Changing Cultures," from the *Tundra Times,* Vol. I, No. 4, November 1962. Published by the Eskimo, Indian, Aleut Publishing Company, Inc., Fairbanks, Alaska. Reprinted by permission.

"On the Art of Stealing Human Rights," from *Akwesasne Notes,* Vol. I, No. 7, July, 1969. Published by the Mohawk Nation at Akwesasne, Roosevelt, New York. Reprinted by permission of the author.

"The New Indian Wars," from *American Aborigine,* National Indian Youth Council, Vol. III, No. 1. Reprinted by permission.

"Which One Are You? Five Types of Young Indians," from an undated pamphlet, Clyde Warrior Institute in American Indian Studies. Reprinted by permission of Mrs. Clyde Warrior.

"Protection Against 'Thinkers'—A Cherokee Chant," from Jack Frederick Kilpatrick and Anna Gritts Kilpatrick, *Run Toward the Nightland* (Dallas: Southern Methodist University Press, 1967). Copyright © 1967 by Southern Methodist University Press and reprinted by permission.

"Too Many Scientists and Not Enough Chiefs," from the *Tundra Times*, August, 1969. Published by the Eskimo, Indian, Aleut Publishing Company, Inc., Fairbanks, Alaska. Reprinted by permission.

"Fourteen Strings of Purple Wampum to Writers About Indians," from *The People*, Vol. I, No. 2, August, 1968: *Six Nations Pamphlets*, Akwesasne Counselor Organization, Hogansburg, New York. Reprinted by permission.

"Open Letter to [Red] Skelton," from *Rosebud Sioux Herald* (*Eyapaha*), Rosebud, South Dakota, Vol. II, No. 14. Reprinted by permission of the author.

"A Word on Indian Studies Programs," from *Akwesasne Notes*, Vol. I, No. 7, July, 1969. Published and reprinted by permission of the Mohawk Nation at Akwesasne, Roosevelt, New York.

"Cultural Factors in the Education of American Indians," from an address given at the 200th Anniversary of Dartmouth College, May, 1969. Reprinted by permission of Robert L. Bennett, Director, American Indian Law Center, University of New Mexico, Albuquerque, New Mexico.

"Love Poems and Spring Poems and Dream Poems and War Poems," from Gerald Vizenor, *Anishinabe Nagamon* (Minnesota: Nodin Press, 1965). Reprinted by permission.

"Snow the Last," from Joseph L. Concha, *Lonely Deer: Poems by a Pueblo Boy* (Taos, New Mexico: Taos Pueblo Council, 1969). Reprinted by permission of the author.

"Grandfather and I," "A New Visitor," from *Feathered Words*, Taos Pueblo Day School, Spring and Winter, 1969. Reprinted by permission of the author.

"In One Day My Mother Grew Old," from *Drumbeats*, Institute of American Indian Arts, Santa Fe, New Mexico, Vol. II, No. 5, April, 1969. Reprinted by permission.

"Untitled," by Vance Good Iron, from *Akwesasne Notes,* Vol. I, No. 7, July, 1969. Published and reprinted by permission of the Mohawk Nation at Akwesasne, Roosevelt, New York.

"The Man from Washington," from John R. Milton, editor, *The American Indian Speaks* (Vermillion, South Dakota: University of South Dakota Press, 1969). Reprinted by permission.

"One Chip of Human Bone," from *Pembroke Magazine,* Pembroke State University, North Carolina, 1971. Reprinted by permission.

"Three Poems," by Calvin O'John, from *The Writers' Reader,* Spring, 1964, Institute of American Indian Arts, Santa Fe, New Mexico. Reprinted by permission.

"It Is Not!" and "I Am a Papago Girl," from *The New Trail,* 1953 School Yearbook of the Phoenix Indian School, Phoenix, Arizona. Reprinted by permission.

"Walk Proud, Walk Straight, Let Your Thoughts Race," and "When I Was Young, My Father Said," from Sixth Annual Vincent Price Awards in Creative Writing, Institute of American Indian Arts, 1968. Reprinted by permission.

"New Way Old Way," from *The Writers' Reader,* Institute of American Indian Arts, Santa Fe, New Mexico, 1964. Reprinted by permission.

"Death," from *The New Trail,* 1953 School Yearbook of the Phoenix Indian School, Phoenix, Arizona. Reprinted by permission.

"My Life," from *Akwesasne Notes,* Vol. I, No. 7, July, 1969. Published and reprinted by permission of the Mohawk Nation at Akwesasne, Roosevelt, New York.

"War Signs," from *The Writers' Reader,* Institute of American Indian Arts, Santa Fe, New Mexico, Spring, 1964.

"Poem for Vietnam," from *Pembroke Magazine,* Pembroke State University, North Carolina, 1971. Reprinted by permission.

"Youth Dies of Exposure" and "Three Kayenta Teachers Resign," from *Navajo Times,* January 29, 1970. Reprinted by permission.

"A Navajo Medicine Man Cures His Son," from Sidney M. Callaway, Gary Witherspoon, *et al., Grandfather Stories* (Rough Rock, Arizona: Navajo Curriculum Center, 1970). Reprinted by permission.

"We Gave Them Meat, They Gave Us Poison," from Wilcomb E. Washburn, editor, *The Indian and the White Man* (New York: Doubleday and Co., 1964). Copyright © 1964 by Wilcomb E. Washburn. Reprinted by permission of Doubleday and Co., Inc.

The Missionary in a Cultural Trap, from a privately issued manuscript, undated. Reprinted by permission of the author.

"Religion of the People," from a mimeographed paper, undated. Reprinted by permission of the author.

"Oath of Office of the Pueblos," from *The Indian Historian*, Vol. II, No. 3, Fall, 1969. Reprinted by permission of the translator, Joe Sando.

"The Laws of the Indians," from *Great Plains Observer*, January, 1969. Reprinted by permission.

"Law of the Outlaws," from Jack Frederick Kilpatrick and Anna Gritts Kilpatrick, *Run Toward the Nightland* (Dallas: Southern Methodist University Press, 1967). Copyright © 1967 by Southern Methodist University Press and reprinted by permission.

"A Death in South Dakota," from *Rosebud Sioux Herald* (*Eyapaha*), Rosebud, South Dakota, October 20, 1969. Reprinted by permission.

"On Death Row," from Gerald Vizenor, *Thomas James White Hawk* (Minnesota: Four Winds Press, 1968). Reprinted by permission of Gerald Vizenor.

"A Soldier Must Do Battle," and "Should Indians Fight in 'White Man's War?'" from *Navajo Times*, April 2, 1970. Reprinted by permission.

"Navajo Banished to Reservation," from *Maine Indian Newsletter*, Vol. III, No. 10, June, 1969, Old Town, Maine. Reprinted by permission.

"I Choose to Serve My People," from *Renegade*, published by Survival of American Indian Association, Vol. I, No. 1. Reprinted by permission.

"The Voice of the American Indian, Declaration of Indian Purpose," from *The Voice of the American Indian,* American Indian Chicago Conference, Conference papers, University of Chicago, June, 1961. Reprinted by permission of Dr. Sol Tax.

"Red Power: An Eight Point Program," from *Akwesasne Notes*, Vol. I, No. 5, May, 1969. Published and reprinted by permission of the Mohawk Nation at Akwesasne, Roosevelt, New York.

"Okla-Houma: The Red-Earth-Colored-People," from United Native Americans, *Warpath*, Vol. I, No. 1, Summer, 1968. Reprinted by permission.

"The Warriors of the Rainbow," from William Willoya and Vinson Brown, *Warriors of the Rainbow* (Healdsburg, California: Naturegraph Company, 1952). Reprinted by permission of the publishers.

"So Let There Be Happiness," from *The New Trail*, 1953 School Yearbook of the Phoenix Indian School, Phoenix, Arizona. Reprinted by permission.

A NOTE ON THE TYPE

This book was set in Laurel, a phototype-
setting version of Caledonia, designed by
W. A. Dwiggins. It belongs to the family of
printing types called "modern face" by
printers—a term used to mark the change
in style of type letters that occurred about
1800. It borders on the general design of
Scotch Modern, but is more freely drawn
than that letter.

*This book was composed, printed and
bound by The Colonial Press Inc., Clinton,
Massachusetts. Typography and binding
design by* CLINT ANGLIN.